Gu

GW00720650

Commissioned by **David Spriggs;** *Edited by* **Lisa Cherrett**

Guidelines © BRF 2015

The Bible Reading Fellowship

15 The Chambers, Vineyard, Abingdon OX14 3FE

Tel: 01865 319700; Fax: 01865 319701

E-mail: enquiries@brf.org.uk; Websites: www.brf.org.uk; www.biblereadingnotes.org.uk

ISBN 978 0 85746 124 7

Distributed in Australia by Mediacom Education Inc., PO Box 610, Unley, SA 5061.

Tel: 1800 811 311; Fax: 08 8297 8719;

E-mail: admin@mediacom.org.au

Available also from all good Christian bookshops in Australia.

For individual and group subscriptions in Australia:

Mrs Rosemary Morrall, PO Box W35, Wanniassa, ACT 2903.

Distributed in New Zealand by Scripture Union Wholesale, PO Box 760, Wellington

Tel: 04 385 0421; Fax: 04 384 3990; E-mail: suwholesale@clear.net.nz

Publications distributed to more than 60 countries

Acknowledgments

Printed by Gutenberg Press, Tarxien, Malta.

Suggestions for using *Guidelines*

Set aside a regular time and place, if possible, when you can read and pray undisturbed. Before you begin, take time to be still and, if you find it helpful, use the BRF prayer.

In *Guidelines*, the introductory section provides context for the passages or themes to be studied, while the units of comment can be used daily, weekly, or whatever best fits your timetable. You will need a Bible (more than one if you want to compare different translations) as Bible passages are not included. At the end of each week is a 'Guidelines' section, offering further thoughts about, or practical application of what you have been studying.

Occasionally, you may read something in *Guidelines* that you find particularly challenging, even uncomfortable. This is inevitable in a series of notes which draws on a wide spectrum of contributors, and doesn't believe in ducking difficult issues. Indeed, we believe that *Guidelines* readers much prefer thought-provoking material to a bland diet that only confirms what they already think.

If you do disagree with a contributor, you may find it helpful to go through these three steps. First, think about why you feel uncomfortable. Perhaps this is an idea that is new to you, or you are not happy at the way something has been expressed. Or there may be something more substantial— you may feel that the writer is guilty of sweeping generalisation, factual error, theological or ethical misjudgment. Second, pray that God would use this disagreement to teach you more about his word and about yourself. Third, think about what you will do as a result of the disagreement. You might resolve to find out more about the issue, or write to the contributor or the editors of *Guidelines*.

To send feedback, you may email or write to BRF at the addresses shown opposite. If you would like your comment to be included on our website, please email connect@brf.org.uk. You can also Tweet to @brfonline, using the hashtag #brfconnect.

Writers in this issue

Paula Gooder is Theologian in Residence for the Bible Society. Her specialism is St Paul, particularly 2 Corinthians, but she has a strong and abiding love for the Gospels—especially the Gospel of Mark. She lives in Birmingham with her husband and two daughters.

David Spriggs has retired from Bible Society but continues his work with them as a consultant. His main role is as a team minister at the Hinckley Baptist Church, where he has special responsibility to work with the leaders.

Steve Walton is Research Fellow at St Mary's University College, Twickenham, and Honorary Research Fellow at Tyndale House, Cambridge. He is an Anglican priest and has written a number of books and articles. He is presently working on a major commentary on Acts.

Derek Tidball is a Baptist minister, author and speaker, who was principal of London School of Theology and is currently visiting scholar at Spurgeon's College, London.

Margaret Guite is an Anglican priest. During the 1980s she taught Doctrine in two colleges of the Cambridge Theological Federation. Since then she has been serving in various parishes in the Diocese of Ely and is currently parish priest of St Mark's, Cambridge, and an honorary canon of Ely. She is married with two grown-up children.

David Ball is Director of Open Learning at Trinity College, Bristol. He was born in Kenya, where his parents were missionaries. David studied Biblical Studies at Sheffield University, where he also did his PhD.

Oldi Morava is currently working with Bible Society to translate the Old Testament into Albanian as part of an interconfessional team. He graduated from Redcliffe College with a BA in Applied Theology and later completed a Masters in Biblical Hebrew at Oxford University. He is married with one daughter.

P.W. (Bill) Goodman is a teacher, writer and Anglican clergyman living in Leicestershire. He loves helping people explore the Bible in different cultural contexts. His PhD set contemporary songs in conversation with biblical songs.

The Editor writes...

Holidays may take us to new places or old haunts. I've just come back from revisiting well-known places in Devon, which is probably why this image comes to mind. This issue of *Guidelines* contains some familiar passages, but our expert writers guide us into new insights. While on holiday I also discovered stately homes and gardens that were new to me; equally, there are less well-known biblical books to consider.

We begin with Paula Gooder and the first half of the Gospel of Mark. Paula's ability to bring the best of contemporary scholarship, combined with a deep faith, is modelled well in these first three weeks' notes.

In other New Testament studies, Derek Tidball has gathered some key passages from the first three Gospels about the kingdom of God —a topic that was central to the life and ministry of Jesus. David Ball focuses on the place of the cross and resurrection in the Gospel of John and so offers us helpful preparation for the events of Holy Week.

Steve Walton has spent many years researching and teaching the Acts of the Apostles. Now we can benefit from his expert knowledge as he moves us swiftly through the first half of this book, which is so important for us as we seek to understand the good news of Jesus in a constantly changing cultural landscape.

One of the liveliest, most puzzling of Paul's letters is 1 Corinthians. Again, this is vital biblical material for us in our increasingly pagan, multi-religious environment. Bill Goodman brings the historical and contemporary situations together, reminding us of the core gospel message as well as the complex societal challenges that the church faces.

The New Testament is built on the foundations of the Old, and the deceptively simple story of Ruth provides us with a clear example of this. Oldi Morava, a Bible translator, shares some of his specialist knowledge of this enchanting book. Many people struggle with the pessimism and apparent confusions of Ecclesiastes, yet this book, too, is a vital contribution to the whole canon of scripture. It is good to welcome Margaret Guite back to help us through its challenges and insights.

Finally I explore the book of Hosea—one of the earliest 'writing' prophets. Within these few pages we can sense the cost of ministry as, together, Hosea and God seek to alert his people who are succumbing to the pressures of their culture.

I pray that you will enjoy your scriptural tour through *Guidelines* and that your faith will be strengthened for your spiritual journey.

David Spriggs

The BRF Prayer

Almighty God,
you have taught us that your word is a lamp for our
feet and a light for our path. Help us, and all who
prayerfully read your word, to deepen our
fellowship with you and with each other through your love.
And in so doing may we come to know you more fully,
love you more truly, and follow more faithfully in
the steps of your son Jesus Christ, who lives and
reigns with you and the Holy Spirit,
one God for evermore. Amen.

Mark 1:1—8:21

Mark's Gospel is the most vivid of all the Gospels. Its pace is quick, its style is clear and it is easy to read. Indeed, of all the Gospels, Mark's especially appears intended to be read in a single sitting. The major focus of the Gospel—discipleship and its cost—becomes clear when you read all 16 chapters together. This does not mean that it cannot also be read more slowly and savoured but it is worth reading it through in one go before going back and reading again, more slowly, as this will help you to hold the whole sweep of the story in your mind.

There are various possible ways to see the structure of Mark's Gospel, but the easiest (and the one that fits best with looking at chapters 1—8) is to split it into four sections:

- Mark 1:2—4:34: Introducing the life and ministry of Jesus
- Mark 4:35—8:38: The nature of discipleship
- Mark 9:1—10:52: The cost of discipleship
- Mark 11:1—16:8: The way of the cross

Under this structure, the first eight chapters introduce us to the key themes of Mark's Gospel, which then unfold further in the second eight chapters.

Mark 1:2—4:34 acts as an introduction to the life and ministry of Jesus. Each of these four chapters includes at least one of some of the most crucial aspects of Jesus ministry: the calling of disciples, the driving out of unclean spirits, healings, conflict with the Jewish authorities, teachings and parables. They set the scene for who Jesus is and what his ministry will be like. Chapters 4—8 focus much more on the nature and challenge of discipleship and raise the question of what the proper response is to Jesus.

Mark's Gospel is thought by most New Testament scholars to have been the first Gospel written (in either the late 60s or early 70s AD) and to have been used as one source among others by both Matthew and Luke when they then wrote their Gospels. It certainly has the feel of an eyewitness account. Christian tradition associates this narrative with Peter, who passed it on to someone called Mark.

Quotations are taken from the New Revised Standard Version of the Bible.

1 The beginning of the good news

Mark 1:1

Mark's Gospel, unlike the others, rather bursts in on us. No sooner has Mark declared the beginning of the Gospel than we are introduced to John the Baptist and his baptising in the river Jordan, and the story takes off. Indeed, it barely pauses for breath until, just as abruptly, it ends with the women at the tomb being afraid and running away. This causes us to pause for a moment and reflect on the opening verse. There are only four elements in this verse: beginning, good news, Jesus Christ and Son of God, and yet they are all, in their way, significant. We will begin at the end.

It may be that the final element, 'Son of God', shouldn't actually be here. Some of the earliest manuscripts do not contain the phrase 'Son of God' and some critics suggest that it has been added later. This may be the case, but, if it was added in, it is for a good reason: 'Jesus Christ, Son of God' tells us almost as much as we need to know about this character. His name, Jesus, means 'saviour'. 'Christ', as many of you will know, is the Greek translation of 'Messiah', and 'Son of God' describes his relationship with God. So here we encounter the Saviour, Messiah and child of God, and we are set up to understand who this Jesus is whom we are about to meet.

The really interesting bit of the phrase, though, is 'beginning of the good news'. The first thing to notice is that in Greek there is no 'the' before 'beginning'. This makes the opening words even more abrupt. The question is: what is the beginning?

Obviously this verse marks the beginning of Mark's account but we don't really need to be told this: we could have worked it out for ourselves. This suggests that the opening verse is telling us that the Gospel itself is the beginning of the good news. In other words, the good news does not end with the Gospel. The Gospel is only a beginning: the rest of the story is lived out in the lives of us, its readers. This may be the beginning of good news but it is not the whole story.

2 Baptism for repentance

As we have noticed already, the pace of Mark's Gospel is such that it has barely begun before we meet John the Baptist. A disruptive, disreputable prophet-like figure suddenly appears in the wilderness proclaiming 'a baptism of repentance for the forgiveness of sins' (v. 4).

This whole episode is rich with meaning—a meaning that can be easy for us, in the 21st century, to miss. Mark sets up the significance of the event by claiming to quote from the prophet Isaiah. In fact, he is quoting from both Malachi and Isaiah: verse 2 comes from Malachi 3:1 and verse 3 from Isaiah 40:3. In their original contexts, both verses herald the return of God to his people so that he can lead them home from exile in Babylon. For this to happen, preparation was needed. The people needed to be ready to greet God on his return and the way for his return needed to be smoothed and prepared.

The best place for this preparation to happen was the wilderness—but not just any old wilderness. The place where John was to be found was the wilderness by the River Jordan—in other words, the place where Joshua and the people of God had entered the land the first time. The people needed to begin again and, from that new beginning, to be ready to greet God as he returned.

This is why John's baptism of repentance for the forgiveness of sins was so important. Ritual cleansing with water was common in first-century Judaism. Male Jews cleansed themselves every time they went into the temple. The difference between John's baptism and ritual cleansing was that, in ritual cleansing, you cleansed yourself; with John's baptism, someone else cleansed you. This made the cleansing both public and community based. It required people to join together publicly, to let go of everything that had happened in the past and, together, to wait, prepared for God's return to his people.

3 My beloved Son

The next scene of Mark's Gospel introduces us to a theme that runs through the whole Gospel. John and the people from Jerusalem are in the wilderness, on the banks of the River Jordan, preparing themselves to greet God on his return to his people. The question that hangs in the air is: will they be able to recognise Jesus when he comes?

The way in which Mark tells the story here leaves the question open. In 1:7–8, John the Baptist has declared that there is someone coming after him who is more powerful than him, whose sandals he is not worthy to untie, but Mark does not tell us whether, in fact, John does recognise Jesus when he baptises him, or not. In John's Gospel (1:15), John the Baptist recognises him straight away, but Mark leaves the question open.

This is for a good reason. One of Mark's main themes is the question of who will recognise 'Jesus Christ, Son of God' for who he really is. The good news that he has announced in his opening verse is good news only if it is recognised as such. The key question of the Gospel is: who will recognise Jesus for who he is and what are the circumstances that will allow them to do so?

Jesus' baptism initiates this theme not only by leaving open the question of whether John the Baptist recognises him but also by making God's pronouncement about Jesus private. In Mark, as Jesus comes out of the water, the heavens are torn apart, the Spirit descends like a dove and God speaks, declaring Jesus to be his beloved Son (vv. 10–11), but the way it is told implies that only Jesus sees the dove and hears God's voice. Jesus knows that he is God's Son; we, the readers, know it too, but it is unclear whether the rest of the people have heard it. They are left to work it out for themselves, the hard way.

The narrative of the rest of the Gospel focuses our attention on the question of who will be able to recognise and respond to Jesus for who he really is.

4 Come, follow me

Mark 1:14–28

One of the striking features of Mark's Gospel is that in it we meet people both in groups and as individuals. In this passage we meet two of the three key groups in the Gospel (the third is introduced at the start of Mark 2). The first group is the disciples, and here Jesus calls the first of them: Simon, Andrew, James and John. The disciples are an intriguing group in Mark's Gospel. They hear Jesus' call and immediately get up, leave everything and follow him (vv. 18, 20); so far, so good. They also remain faithful to him throughout the whole of his ministry—at least until his arrest—but at the same time they seem to struggle to comprehend who he is and what he has come to do, as we shall see in the next few chapters.

The second group is the crowd, whom we meet for the first time in verse 27. Here, they are as they remain throughout the majority of the Gospel—amazed. The crowd, it seems, follow Jesus with their mouths constantly hanging open in astonishment. Jesus is like nobody they have ever encountered before, and so they follow him and are amazed by him, but, it appears, cannot offer any greater response than that. The crowd, as a group, are intrigued by Jesus, fascinated by him, but are not able to follow him as the disciples do, or respond to him as he really is.

These two groups contrast sharply with the individuals who meet Jesus along the way. The first of these, the man with an unclean spirit, knows exactly who Jesus is—the Holy One of God. Not only does he know, but he shouts about it at the top of his voice (v. 24). It is slightly surprising, then, that Jesus tells him to be quiet (v. 25). Surely the unclean spirit is right and should be congratulated? It is here that we encounter another of Mark's themes—a theme that, over the years, has been called 'the messianic secret'. Over and over again, to our surprise, Jesus tells all sorts of people *not* to proclaim who he is. The question for us to explore as we read through Mark is: why did he do this?

5 The Jesus who heals

Mark 1:29—2:12

In this very next story we find a partial answer to the question of why Jesus told people not to proclaim who he was: he very quickly became a celebrity. In verse 33 the whole city of Capernaum is said to be gathered at Jesus' door, and at the start of Mark 2 the house is so crowded with people that a paralysed man has to be let down through the roof to reach him. Between these two events, Jesus heals a leper and, again, tells him not to say anything, but instead the man goes around telling everyone. This severely curtails Jesus' ministry and 1:45 reports that it means he is no longer able to go into towns openly.

One of the reasons why Jesus was so keen that people should not proclaim what he had done was because of their tendency to get the wrong end of the stick. As is apparent from even the first two chapters of Mark, the people very quickly came to see Jesus as a convenient wonder-worker. The problem was that healing people was not the main focus of Jesus' ministry. His main focus, as Mark 1:15 made clear, was to proclaim that the kingdom of God was at hand and that people needed to be ready (as John the Baptist, too, had told them to be) to welcome the kingdom of God when it broke in. Jesus himself identifies this as the main focus of his ministry in 1:38, but the more well known he became for healing, the less able he was to do what he had really come to do—proclaim the kingdom of God.

Part of the reason why Jesus was so eager to keep people quiet about the healings he had done was that they might end up understanding only half of who he was—the half about his ability to heal people. As a result, they risked preventing him from proclaiming the whole message of God's disturbing, challenging kingdom breaking forth on earth.

6 A disruptive presence

Mark 2:13–28

Another of the major features of Mark's account is that he brings out just how unsettling and disturbing Jesus and his message were. This passage describes a string of ways in which Jesus disconcerted people: he called a tax collector to follow him, he didn't fast with his disciples like John the Baptist did, and he plucked grain on the sabbath. To us, these actions might seem to be small and unimportant, but to Mark and his audience they represented a refusal to go along with expectations simply for the sake of it.

The reason for Jesus' breaking with expectations is different in each case. Starting with the final example and moving backwards: the plucking of grain was deemed by the Pharisees to be 'work' and therefore should not have been done on the sabbath. The point that Jesus makes, however, is that the sabbath is a gift to us from God: it was made for us; we were not made for the sabbath. Therefore, sabbath rules should be for our benefit, not to do us harm.

In the case of fasting, this was something you did to clear your thoughts as you waited for God (the bridegroom). Jesus' disciples had no need to wait for God as he was already with them. The time might come when fasting would be needed again, but it was unnecessary at this time.

In the question of Jesus' mixing with tax collectors and sinners, it is very clear what is going on. The group loosely called 'tax collectors and sinners' were outcasts from society. Their behaviour, including their willingness to work for the Roman empire, meant that they were shunned at all costs—but Jesus did not shun them. He spent time with them, talking and eating with them.

We discover, therefore, a theme running through all three of these seemingly random incidents. People were making unthinking assumptions—that those whom society deemed to be outcasts should be treated as such; that all disciples of a rabbi should fast as a matter of course; that if you should not 'work' on the sabbath, this meant doing nothing at all, even if it was detrimental to health and well-being. Jesus' disruptive presence took the form of drawing people back to think again about a whole range of issues and people.

Guidelines

One of the themes that has arisen very powerfully in these opening chapters of Mark's Gospel is the theme of response to Jesus. So far, we have encountered a range of responses, from the very closed-minded antagonism of the Pharisees to the open-mouthed amazement of the crowd; from the immediate following of Jesus by Simon, Andrew, James and John to the loud and fearful shrieking of his identity by the unclean spirit. The very person of Jesus—who he was, and what he said and did—evoked a reaction.

The question that Mark's Gospel poses time and time again is: how will we respond? Most people reading these notes will have already responded to Jesus in some way—it is unlikely that they would be reading these notes otherwise—but Mark's Gospel presses us further. An initial response is one thing; ongoing response is another. Perhaps we tend to domesticate Jesus, to make him into 'gentle Jesus, meek and mild', but he is not, and never was, that person. Jesus is and always has been a disruptive, questing, questioning presence whose very being demands that we venture with him to places we never dreamed of going. The question is: how will you respond?

1 Purity versus love

Mark 3:1–19a

It is very easy to dismiss the Pharisees in Mark's Gospel. They appear almost like pantomime villains, hanging around, daring Jesus to cross them and waiting to find fault with him. They appear in this passage in exactly that guise, almost willing Jesus to do something that will give them cause to hate him.

It is important, however, to know a little about the Pharisees, as it can help us understand them better. The Pharisees appear to have emerged as a group during the time after Judas Maccabeus and his followers had driven the Greek empire out of Judea (c. 163BC). Although at first they had both religious and political influence, by the time of Jesus only their religious influence was surviving. It is important to know that they were representatives of a popular lay movement (not members of the temple priesthood) who believed that the standards of purity expected of priests in the temple should be observed by everyone in their everyday lives. In other words, they were a popular pietistic movement who were concerned with the way ordinary people might worship God properly.

This is probably why they came into conflict with Jesus so often. Jesus also pointed to a way to worship God properly, but it was very different from the way of the Pharisees. The Pharisees believed that God would be worshipped best when the purity laws were followed as closely as possible and everyone lived as though they were priests. Jesus believed that God would be worshipped best when God's love was shown to everyone, no matter who they were, as clearly and as often as possible. The healing of a man on the sabbath was a classic moment at which the principles of the Pharisees and those of Jesus clashed. The Pharisees fell back on a proper interpretation of the law and Jesus fell back on the principle of love.

It would not be right to condemn the Pharisees outright. They were simply trying to worship God to the best of their capacity. The problem was that, in their concern to obey the rules, they lost sight of the needs of human beings. Rather than condemning them, we should think long and hard about those times in our own lives when, from the best of motives, we too have lost sight of the needs of those around us.

2 Families and sinning against the Holy Spirit

Mark 3:19b–35

The saying in this passage about the sin against the Holy Spirit which will never be forgiven (vv. 28–29) probably troubles people more than any other of Jesus' sayings. There are some who agonise over what it could be that will never be forgiven, as opposed to the many other sins and blasphemies that they might commit or utter, which will be forgiven. In reality, this passage is not at all hard to interpret, so long as you read Jesus' saying about the Holy Spirit in the context in which it appears. Most people take it out of its context and hence feel bemused about its meaning.

Jesus makes this utterance in response to the scribes from Jerusalem who attributed his ability to cast out demons to the power of Beelzebul (v. 22). Beelzebul (which, in other ancient manuscripts, is written as Beelzebub) appears to be a popular name for Satan, and Mark certainly makes this connection in verses 22–23. The scribes' argument is that because

Jesus can communicate with evil spirits that come from the devil, he must be one of them himself; Jesus counters this with the argument that he has power to cast out the evil spirits and therefore cannot be considered to be one of them (a logical statement indeed!). He then goes on to talk about the blasphemy against the Holy Spirit. In this context, Jesus clearly means that those who deliberately and consistently confuse what comes from God with what comes from the devil are sinning against God's own Holy Spirit. Those who declare what is good to be evil, and what is from God to be from the devil, are those who commit such a sin. His meaning, then, appears clear, and his message is a powerful warning to us all to take great care about what we declare to be evil.

In a way, it is odd that people focus on this saying of Jesus, when his next words (vv. 33–35) are, in many ways, more disturbing. In this discussion about families, Jesus declares that, in his kingdom, his family encompasses whoever does the will of God. In other words, our own biological families are less important than God's family. If we are to feel troubled by any of Jesus' teaching, I would suggest that this is far more troubling than his teaching on the sin against the Holy Spirit.

3 Everything comes in parables

Mark 4:1–34

It is often noted that Mark includes much less of what Jesus said in his teachings than either Matthew or Luke do. For example, Mark's Gospel does not have an equivalent of the Sermon on the Mount (Matthew 5—7) or the Sermon on the Plain (Luke 6:20–49) and, although Mark often says that Jesus taught, he doesn't always tell us what he said. Here in chapter 4 we hear for the first time some content of Jesus' teaching, and it is very important to notice that it comes in a variety of parables—first the parable of the sower (vv. 1–20), then the parable of the lamp on the lampstand (vv. 21–25), then another parable about sowing (vv. 26–29) and finally the parable of the mustard seed (vv. 30–33).

The only parable that is explained in Mark's Gospel is the first of these—the parable of the sower. As a result, it appears to be a parable about parables, explaining why it is that some people do not understand

Jesus' teaching. It is because, as Jesus explains in verses 14–20, some have the word taken from them immediately; in others, the word has no root and cannot survive; others find the word choked by the cares of the world. Only a few hear the word, have it take root in them and bear fruit. Whether or not the other parables in chapter 4 will be understood or not will depend largely on the kind of person who hears them.

Verses 1–20, then, make up a very important passage for understanding the responses to Jesus that we encounter throughout the Gospel. Jesus has given us a way of making sense of why some people recognise him and others don't: they will only recognise him if they are 'good soil' people. If they are not 'good soil', they will not be able to make sense of who he is and what he does. Jesus confirms this in verses 11–12: he teaches in parables precisely so that 'good soil' people will hear, respond and understand, while 'path', 'rocky soil' and 'weedy soil' people will find themselves unable to comprehend. Jesus' teaching is the means by which we discover what kind of people we and others are. It is important not just for what Jesus says but also for what it reveals about who we are.

4 Have you still no faith?

Mark 4.34–41

Mark 4:35 seems to open a new section of Mark's Gospel. Mark 1:2—4:34 is, as we noted earlier, a scene-setting section. In it we have been introduced to Jesus' life and ministry through a number of healings, teachings and even conflicts. From 4:35 onwards, our attention is focused much more closely on two key themes: the disciples and their response to Jesus, and Jesus' healings of various 'outsiders' like the Syro-Phoenician woman and the Gerasene demoniac. You will notice that the passage set for today begins not at 4:35 but at 4:34, because the final verse of Mark's first section is important for understanding what is going on in the whole of this second section. In 4:34 Mark tells us that Jesus did not talk to the 'outsiders' except in parables, but that he explained everything to his disciples in private. We begin this section, therefore, expecting the disciples, unlike everyone else, to understand who Jesus is and what he has come to do.

This brings us to the story of the stilling of the storm at the end of chapter 4, and very quickly we discover that any expectations we might have had about the disciples' comprehension of Jesus' identity are not to be fulfilled. In all fairness, I would be with the disciples! They are in the midst of a great storm, Jesus is apparently completely unaware of the danger they are facing, and they panic. Jesus' question to the disciples seems unfair in the extreme: 'Why are you afraid?' 'Well, because there is a great storm and we think we are going to die' would be an obvious answer. However, that question is not quite what Jesus asks. The usual Greek word for being afraid is not used here; instead, we find the word *deilos*, which means 'timid' or 'cowardly'.

In other words, Jesus is not asking, 'Why were you afraid in this one instance?' He is asking, 'Why are you so often afraid? Why do you have the characteristic of fear?' His next question, 'Have you still no faith?' implies that having faith will stop them being so timid, and this is a good introduction to the next major section in Mark. We need to recognise that being a disciple of Jesus is not just an intellectual exercise. Jesus may explain everything to his disciples in private but the response he expects of them is transformation, not just comprehension.

5 How much the Lord has done for you

Mark 5:1–20

The story of the healing of the man from the Gerasene area is justifiably well known due to its spectacular nature, but it is also vital to the unfolding of Mark's story at this point in the Gospel.

It is not easy to identify where this miracle took place, not least because there are variants of the placename in different Gospel manuscripts (other possibilities including Gergesenes and Gadarenes). The differences have arisen probably because Gerasa was 30 miles from Lake Galilee and later scribes have tried to offer suggestions of places closer to the shoreline (note vv. 1–2). It may be that Mark himself had a rather hazy knowledge of geography and did not realise he was referring to the wrong place.

Much more important than this, however, is that the miracle comes directly after the stilling of the storm in the previous chapter. Both stories contain chaos and fear, which are transformed into calmness and peace. Just as the lake was 'dead calm' in 4:39, so the man is 'clothed and in his right mind' in 5:15. Just as fear was present in the boat, so the people are afraid in 5:15. The placing of these two stories next to each other stresses the connections between them and illustrates that Jesus has authority over all forces that bring chaos in the world, whether they be natural phenomena or evil spirits.

The intriguing difference between the two stories, however, is the nature of the fear that is described. As we noted above, the disciples were chastised by Jesus for being timid but the people from the Gerasene area were not. In addition, the disciples were afraid before Jesus acted, whereas the people in this story were afraid after he had healed the man. This tells us that Jesus had different expectations of his disciples from those he had of others. He expected the disciples to comprehend who he was, but he had no such expectation of the people from Gerasa, whose misunderstanding caused them to fear the very person who could save them.

6 Outsiders and an insider

Mark 5:21–43

As we progress through this part of Mark's Gospel, we meet a string of people who encounter Jesus in different ways. Nearly all of these people are outsiders in the society in which they live. In the previous passage there was a man possessed by demons and living among the tombs. Here we meet a woman who is haemorrhaging—a condition that would have rendered her ritually unclean and unable to mix freely with the people around her. Later, Jesus engages with a Gentile woman (7:25–30), a man who is deaf and has a speech impediment (7:32–37) and a blind man (8:22–26). All of them, in their way, are forced to be outsiders either because they are Gentiles or because they are ill (or, in the case of the man from Gerasa, both).

Jairus, then, is prominent as the odd one out. As the leader of the synagogue, he is an important insider with influence and power. Indeed, in

Mark, he is the only Jewish leader who responds positively to Jesus. What he has in common with all the other individuals whom Jesus encounters is that, like them, he really needs Jesus' help. Without Jairus in the group, we might think that the necessary condition for genuine response to Jesus, in Mark, is that the person concerned should be an outsider. Jairus shows us that the condition is to be someone who clearly and genuinely sees their need of the help that only Jesus can offer.

The New English Bible translates the beatitude in Matthew 5:3 (normally translated 'Blessed are the poor in spirit') as 'Blessed are those who know their need of God; the kingdom of heaven is theirs'. Although not very close to the original Greek, this translation seems to sum up well the point Mark is making here. The difference between the Jewish leaders as a group and Jairus as an individual is that Jairus knew how much he needed Jesus' help. Mark emphasises the point by wrapping this story around the story of the woman with the haemorrhage, a woman who also was desperate in her illness and loneliness and reached out to Jesus from that desperation.

The Jesus we meet in Mark's Gospel is one who reaches out to those around him; but, as we see time and time again, it is only those who truly know their need of him who are able to recognise him.

Guidelines

As we have journeyed further through Mark, the theme of response to Jesus has remained and deepened. The readings this week have contrasted different people's responses to Jesus, from the Pharisees, with their horrified judgement of Jesus for breaking sabbath law, to Jairus and the haemorrhaging woman, who reached out to Jesus from the depths of their despair. The key difference is that Jairus and the woman with the haemorrhage knew how great their need of Jesus was, whereas the Pharisees lived in confident assurance that they did not, in fact, need him at all.

This is not all. Another contrast can be seen between Jesus' response to those in need of him and to the disciples. Jesus' reprimand to the disciples after the stilling of the storm can sound overly harsh, but what it seems to illustrate is that he has high expectation of discipleship. He does not want or expect his disciples to continue to reach out to him desperately and timidly but, rather, to grow in their discipleship with confidence. Reaching out is a good start but there is much more to our life with Jesus than that.

1 He begins to send them out

Mark 6:1–13

The last time we encountered the disciples in any depth, they were in a boat on the lake, trembling with fear. Now Jesus has called them and sent them out to proclaim that everyone should repent. In our modern age of training courses and certificates, this mission seems premature in the extreme. Jesus has just reprimanded the disciples for being timid; only a little later, we will discover that they still do not understand who Jesus is (6:52), and yet he is already sending them out to proclaim the good news of the kingdom. This reveals that we might wait too long before declaring ourselves and others 'ready' to proclaim the kingdom. For Jesus, the proclamation of the kingdom is far too important, far too urgent, to wait until the disciples feel ready.

This passage also shows that the proclamation will not be plain sailing. Just as Jesus was not welcomed in his home town (vv. 1–6), so too the disciples will find times when they are not well received (v. 11). Jesus' advice on how to respond in such circumstances is clear-sighted and robust. If they find themselves unwelcome, they should shake the dust off their feet as they leave, as a sign of their rejection. This too is counter-intuitive. A natural response to a lack of welcome is to stay longer and try harder; Jesus makes it very clear that some will respond and some will not, and staying longer will not change this fact.

A final observation on this passage must concern the provisions that the disciples are to take with them for the journey—namely, very little. They may take the clothes they stand up in and a staff, but nothing else. This means that they must throw themselves on the hospitality of the people they meet along the way (a condition that makes the command not to stay where they are unwelcome even more sharp-edged). The life of discipleship is one that requires us to take great risks for the sake of the kingdom: no wonder Jesus made it so clear that being timid is not part of being a disciple.

2 The death of John the Baptist

Mark 6:14–29

The second half of Mark's Gospel (comprising the two main sections that run from 9:1 to 10:52 and from 11:1 to 16:8) is characterised by the shadow of the cross. From 9:1 onwards, it becomes clear that Jesus' death is inevitable and that those who wish to follow him faithfully must also accept the way of the cross. As early as chapter 6, in today's passage, Mark begins to prepare us, his readers, for this theme. We have already encountered John the Baptist and observed his key role as the forerunner of Jesus, and in this story we realise that his message was not the only way in which this role was played out. Here too, in his death, John goes ahead of Jesus. We have already seen the ways in which Jesus ran into conflict with the authorities around him. John the Baptist also provoked conflict with authorities (though, admittedly, different ones from those who opposed Jesus) and in this story we see the outcome. Jesus' death is far from inevitable at this point but, with this story, its shadow begins to fall across his path, a shadow that will get steadily darker and deeper from now on.

One of the questions that tantalise scholars about this narrative is what exactly had upset Herodias so much. The 'Herod' family was corrupt and incestuous. Herodias herself was a granddaughter of Herod the Great. She married one of Herod the Great's sons (Herod II, called Philip, and not to be confused with the Herod Philip who ruled part of Herod's empire at this time) and then divorced him and married Herod Antipas (his half-brother, the 'Herod' in this story). Confused? You should be! Herod the Great had a large number of children by different wives, but Herodias was effectively the half-niece of both of her husbands. If anything, divorce was the least of the family's problems and John the Baptist was not the only person to say so.

The question remains, then, what had upset Herodias so much? It may have been that John's popularity meant that his criticism of Herod was widely heard. It may have been that he spoke out that criticism more clearly and aggressively than others did. But what he said so upset the Herod family that Herodias insisted on his death—a death that, as we noted above, increases the tension in Mark's narrative and begins to point to what might also happen to Jesus.

3 They do not understand

Mark 6:30–56

As we near the end of Mark 6, we come upon the second significant encounter between Jesus and his disciples. This meeting, like the one in chapter 4, occurs in a boat, but this time Jesus is not in the boat with them but is walking on the Sea of Galilee through another storm. In many ways, the second event is like the first: there is a great storm; the disciples, again, are terrified; Jesus, again, calms the storm.

Verse 52 observes that they 'did not understand about the loaves, but their hearts were hardened'. Like the criticism of their fear in 4:40, this seems a somewhat harsh judgement, until we stop and reflect on what is going on in the narrative. We have already noted that Jesus has high expectations of his disciples—expectations that they often fail to reach. The judgement here gives us an insight into his expectations of his followers, which is as important for us to recognise as it was for his first disciples.

The clue given in the text is in the observation that 'their hearts were hardened'. It is important to recognise that the Hebrew view of the world associated the decision-making process with the heart, not the head. Having a hard heart, therefore, meant that it was impossible to perceive God or to change and learn more about him (see, for example, Ephesians 4:18: 'They are darkened in their understanding, alienated from the life of God because of their ignorance and hardness of heart').

In their first encounter with Jesus in a boat, the disciples' timidity was pointed out as a blockage to true discipleship. Here we find a second blockage—the inability to think, to learn and to change as a result of encountering Jesus as he really is. We often forget that the word 'disciple' means 'someone who learns' rather than, as is popularly supposed, 'someone who follows Jesus'. Following Jesus, as the first disciples did, is a good start but that does not make us disciples. What makes us disciples is our ability to learn: by definition, if you don't learn, you are not a disciple. Jesus' frustration with the disciples here can be traced back to the fact that they have seen a remarkable and astounding example of the power of God at the feeding of the 5000 (vv. 35–44) and yet they still appear unable to understand who Jesus is. Our challenge, like theirs, is to become people who can learn of God in our daily lives and hence to be true 'disciples'.

4 Nothing outside can defile

Mark 7:1–23

By now you will be getting used to the rhythms of Mark's Gospel. One of the features of these rhythms is the regular conflict that emerges between Jesus and the authorities of his day. It is hardly surprising, then, that after a spectacular feeding miracle such as we find in the feeding of the 5000, Jesus very quickly meets opposition once more. Again, as before in Mark's Gospel, the conflict is between Jesus and the Pharisees and is caused by a difference of practice between them. We noted above that it is important to recognise that the Pharisees were a popular piety movement whose greatest concern was the proper worship of God. Here again we see how easily this proper devotion can become skewed.

The practice of ritual cleansing remains important within Judaism today. The idea emerged from a desire to bring the purity practices from within the temple into everyday life. Purity in the temple was vitally important, as the Jews believed that it enabled God, in his holiness, to dwell in the temple in the midst of the people. Ritual cleansing caused the people to be pure again, and hand washing before meals, alongside the washing of cooking pots and so on, was what enabled this purity to be achieved.

Jesus' observation in verse 15 is that (as we noticed in chapter 2) the Pharisees have allowed the mechanism of the law to blind them to the truth. Real purity—the kind that God is interested in—comes not from what you do externally but from what you do internally. It is who you are as a person that affects how you live your life. It is easy for us to condemn the Pharisees for so badly misunderstanding the purpose of the law, but we need to ensure that we too are not missing the real message of Jesus here. They did not get it wrong because they were Pharisees but because they relied too heavily on rules, without thinking for themselves about what the rules really meant. The big question we face today is not whether we are in danger of washing our hands too often but whether the rules that we rely on, as we live out our faith, help or hinder our vision of the truth.

5 More outsiders

Mark 7:24–37

We have noticed already, in our journey through Mark to this point, the importance of Jesus' encounters with certain outsiders. Between the first and second boat scenes, Jesus met three individuals—the Gerasene demoniac, Jairus and the woman with a haemorrhage. In today's passage he meets two (a Syro-Phoenician woman and a deaf man) and after a third short boat scene (8:13–21) he will meet one more (a blind man at Bethsaida, 8:22–26). Mark appears to be reminding us of true response to Jesus by laying a true responder alongside the disciples, three times.

The person who stands out most strongly in today's couplet is the Syro-Phoenician woman, whose dignity and faithfulness of response to Jesus are remarkable. By contrast, perhaps the most troubling feature of this passage is Jesus' apparent rudeness to the woman. To be called a dog today is far from flattering, but in Jesus' world it was a terrible insult—though a common one, as Jews often described Gentiles as dogs.

Over the years, scholars have wrestled with this passage endlessly. Some suggest that Jesus was being playful and not rude, others that we cannot tell his tone of voice and that he may have sounded less rude in person. Others argue that his encounter with the Syro-Phoenician woman was, in fact, a learning experience for Jesus himself. Until then, they suggest, he had adopted the usual Jewish response to Gentiles and needed to see that this view was too narrow. Still others maintain that Jesus already knew this, and was giving the woman the chance to demonstrate her understanding of who he was and how he related to those around him.

So disparate are the scholarly views that each one of you will need to make up your own mind on whether Jesus was right or wrong here, playful or serious. Whatever decision you make about Jesus' role, the Syro-Phoenician woman stands out as a person of remarkable vision and courage who shows us something of what true discipleship looks like.

6 Do you not yet understand?

Mark 8:1–21

We end this particular section of Mark's Gospel with an episode that ties together many of the strands that we have explored so far. Once more, Jesus reveals who he is (in the feeding of the 4000, a story very similar to the feeding of the 5000); once more, the Pharisees argue with Jesus; once more, the disciples misunderstand what is going on, and once more Jesus encounters someone in great need and heals them.

The crucial incident takes place, again, in a boat. This time, nothing miraculous takes place on the journey (although Jesus has just fed 4000 people with seven loaves and a few fish), but the conversation between Jesus and the disciples brings to a climax the theme of response to Jesus and the nature of discipleship. In order to understand the significance of what Jesus says here, we need to go back to the parable of the sower in chapter 4. There, Jesus said that the disciples had been given the secret of the kingdom of God but that, for those outside, he spoke everything in parables 'in order that "they may indeed look, but not perceive, and may indeed listen, but not understand; so that they may not turn again and be forgiven"' (4:11–12).

If we compare this wording with what Jesus says to the disciples in 8:17–18, then something important emerges. Jesus asks whether they still do not perceive or understand, and whether they have eyes but fail to see. In other words, it turns out that the disciples are still outsiders, after all. Even though the secret of the kingdom has been given to them, they neither perceive it nor understand it. By contrast, those who start as outsiders—because they are ill, or because they are Gentiles, or something similar—appear to perceive and to understand. In the topsy-turvy world of God's kingdom, insiders turn out to be outsiders and vice versa.

It is worth reminding ourselves, though, that all is not lost. The disciples may not be able to understand at the moment, but the point of discipleship is learning, and it is never too late for learning to begin.

Guidelines

As we leave Mark's Gospel at this point in its story (we will return to it later in the year), there is much left unresolved. The next section of the Gospel turns to the cross and the shadow that it casts, with increasing darkness, not only over the life of Jesus but also over the lives of the disciples. We have discovered thus far that Jesus expects the disciples not to be timid, but to have open hearts and be ready to see, perceive and understand. They must be intrepid learners, always open to the things of God and able to understand what it is that they see and experience.

The next section of the Gospel will introduce us to an even more challenging expectation of disciples—that they will take up their cross and follow. This is why they need to be people of courage and openness: they must have the inner strength to face the ultimate challenge of discipleship and to follow Jesus even to the cross.

Think back over the Jesus we have met so far—the Jesus who performed great miracles, went out of his way to heal and care for people, never feared to oppose religious leaders when he believed them to be wrong, and cajoled and urged his disciples into comprehension and learning, as well as so much more.

What is your heart's response to this Jesus, and what is he calling you to do about it?

FURTHER READING

Elizabeth Malbon, *Hearing Mark: A listener's guide*, Continuum, 2002.

Ben Witherington III, *The Gospel of Mark: A socio-rhetorical commentary*, Eerdmans, 2001.

Tom Wright, *Mark for Everyone*, SPCK, 2001.

Hosea

Hosea is one of the earliest Hebrew prophets for whom we have written records, even though he does not appear in our Bibles until the final prophetic corpus, 'The Book of the Twelve Prophets' (or Minor Prophets). Like Amos, historically he precedes Isaiah, Jeremiah and Ezekiel. Like Amos, too, he spoke initially not to Judah and Jerusalem but to the ten northern tribes, now normally referred to as Israel.

After King Solomon's death, the unrest engendered in Israel by the perceived prejudice against the north and favouritism towards the south led to a rebellion against King Rehoboam, who was Solomon's heir (1 Kings 12). Although this move was apparently supported by prophetic intervention, it led to religious tensions, not only between north and south but also within the hearts of Israelites loyal to the covenant with Yahweh. In order to ensure political and civic separation from Judah, Jeroboam, the first northern king, attempted to provide alternative centres of worship. This left Israel even more vulnerable to the local worship of Baal and Ashterah, which was focused on fertility and, ultimately, self-seeking. The separation from Judah, as well as Israel's geographical proximity to Assyria, left Israel exposed to the imperialist drives of this superpower.

Although this historical background might suggest that Hosea's insights will be irrelevant for us, both the deeply empathetic writing and many of the issues he addresses do, in fact, resonate with today's world. The critique of Israel's institutions, Hosea's evaluation of the heart of the military and political threats and his awareness of human vulnerabilities probe our own situations. Economic thraldom, necessary compromises to maintain our power bases, human unfaithfulness and the deep pain it causes, violence and human suffering are some of these issues. Hosea offers us insights as we attempt to see them through the lens of faith while wrestling to maintain moral and spiritual faithfulness in a changing and complex cultural world.

Quotations are taken from the New Revised Standard Version of the Bible unless stated otherwise.

1 History and 'his story'

Hosea 1

As with many (but not all) of the prophets, the book begins with a section that locates its message in the context of Israel's history (v. 1). It appears to cover a long period of history, from Uzziah to Hezekiah in Judah (791–686BC) and the reign of Jeroboam in Israel (793–753BC). The second timespan locates the prophecies more precisely than the first.

There are two issues to note here. First, although Hosea's prophecy seems to be addressed to the northern kingdom of Israel, it is Judah that is mentioned first in verse 1. This might well indicate that the prophecies were collected, edited or preserved in Judah. So, although God was speaking initially through Hosea to the northern tribes, his message was applicable to the whole of God's people then—and, we might add, to the whole of God's people now. Second, the fact that this book is located in history in this way indicates that although the message had continuing validity (see 14:9), it was necessary to understand it contextually. It was a historically conditioned message. Thus both proper historical critical investigation (to locate it in its own times) and ongoing theological exploration and application are supported by verse 1.

The major part of the chapter, however, is a third-person account of Hosea's marriage to an adulterous wife and the birth of his two sons and one daughter. The names of Hosea's children, like Isaiah's later (Isaiah 8:1–4), are prophetic messages in themselves. The final message is that the covenant is over: 'You are not my people, and I am not your God' (v. 9). Interwoven through this total rejection of the northern kingdom is an affirmation that this judgement does not apply to Judah (v. 7) and the staggering (in the context) promise of a restoration of covenant relationship, land, prosperity and one leader for a united kingdom (vv. 10–11).

This raises the possibility that verses 10–11 were added during the preservation of the text. If so, they are indicative of people who had an 'all-Israel' theology, but probably with northern sympathies, so they could well be a similar group to those who edited the book of Deuteronomy.

2 Divine accusation and appeal

Hosea 2:1–23

This chapter begins with an apparent address by Hosea to his three children about their mother, Gomer, and her appalling behaviour (vv. 1–3), hotly followed by a third-person passage that proclaims his rejection of the children (v. 4). These words may well reflect Hosea's own marital experience, for his marriage is part of his mission and the vehicle for his prophetic message, but we cannot be sure where his personal experience gives way to the application to Israel. Certainly by verse 8 the words are being applied to Israel (note the last line, 'which *they* used for Baal'). This application becomes indubitable by verse 11, where 'her' must apply to Israel and not Gomer. Verse 13 brings a threat of punishment.

The opening words can be understood in a different way, however. They could be God's appeal to Hosea to plead with Israel. The language of adultery was used within ancient Near Eastern treaties for disloyalty by the subject nation. While scholars have recognised that one form of prophetic speech is the 'lawsuit or legal accusation' (Stuart, *Hosea–Jonah*, p. 45), how exactly these 'lawsuits' took place is not totally clear, so there is still room for the element of 'pleading' that involves seeking to change attitudes and behaviour by requesting, deploying different motivational keys, or even cajoling. Understood in this way, we are provided with a perspective on Hosea's task, which we see fulfilled in his prophecy.

From this perspective, it is even more significant that the apparently categorical condemnation threatened in verse 13 is not the end. Given the lawsuit context, the 'guilty' verdict and punishment are now anticipated, but what follows in verses 14–23 is quite different. Here we find various ways of depicting total restoration. The passage begins with historical images of the wilderness and the Valley of Achor (probably the gateway from the wilderness to the Jordan Valley), with a reference to Israel's 'youth', when she responded so willingly after her deliverance from Egypt. (This, of course, is not the only way those 'early days' are viewed: it might be argued that Israel rebelled against God from the start.) Then, moving through covenant relationship language, we move on to images of paradisical prosperity, which pick up on the names of Hosea's children and turn them to positives.

3 The cost of restoration

Chapter 3 provides us with one of the critical enigmas in understanding Hosea's marital relationship and (because this relationship stands as an extended prophetic symbol) his message. Among the many questions posed by scholars are:

- Is this a variant (first-person) account of the event described in chapter 1?
- Alternatively, is it another distinct episode in the relationship between Hosea and Gomer, the wife mentioned in chapter 1? If so, did the events of chapter 3 happen before or after the events of chapter 1?
- Is the woman in chapter 3, in fact, a different person from Gomer? Is this another marriage/relationship that Hosea was involved in?
- If so, did this relationship precede or follow the relationship in chapter 1? (The order of events in the book need not reflect their chronological order.)

Intertwined with the answers to these questions are the various moral stances that people take on issues such as whether or not God would command anyone to marry a prostitute or adulteress, and whether it is possible that God would command Hosea, in effect, to imprison his wife.

To many of these questions we cannot give definitive answers, even though we might like to satisfy our curiosity. It is more appropriate to note that the two chapters have very different foci and purposes. Chapter 1 concentrates on the significance of the naming of the children, and chapter 3 on the process of redemption, picking up on the redemption theme in 2:14–23.

Chapter 3 also links into 4:1–3, enabling us to understand the reason for the enforced sexual abstinence both from cultic prostitution and from normal marital relations. The latter is Hosea's personal prophetic expression of the state of uncleanness in the land, which is reflected politically in the nation's loss of king and priest (3:4), socially in the breakdown of law and order (4:2) and spiritually in the 'mourning' of the land (4:3). Abstinence from prostitution is the necessary condition for Israel to be purified and enabled to return to Yahweh. So, focusing on Hosea's abstinence, which was made necessary by the uncleanness of his wife, enables us to understand the 'punishment' of Israel. Although it entails total devastation, even abandonment by God, it will ultimately bring about cleansing. Israel remains 'as mine' (3:3), and inherent in those simple words is a profound theological understanding of history.

4 'All worship corrupts!'

Hosea 4:4–19

The confrontation of Amos with the priest Amaziah is dramatic and well known (see Amos 7:7–17). Although there is nothing like this in Hosea, his critique of the priesthood (in Hebrew, the singular noun is used, but the referent is likely to be 'priesthood' rather than a specific unnamed priest) is even more devastating: 'I reject you from being a priest to me' (v. 6).

This phrase probably reflects the language of the lawsuit. It sounds like the kind of words a husband might use in a divorce, to reject his wife and annul the marriage. It is a devastating and full separation, leaving the rejected party outcast and vulnerable. We should also note the appropriateness of this sentence. It is *lex talionis*, for the priest has 'rejected [the same root word] knowledge' (v. 6).

'Knowledge' is an important word with wide and deep implications. Hosea 4:1 made the assessment, 'There is no faithfulness or loyalty, and no knowledge of God in the land.' From this we perceive, first, that 'knowledge' means a proper understanding of and relationship with the covenant God, rather than proper adherence to all the minutiae of the sacrificial system. Second, in verse 1 this lack of knowledge was the key indictment against all the people, but now the priests, as those who should communicate a true understanding and sustain the people, 'have rejected knowledge' (v. 6). The heart of the criticism seems to be not that they have failed to teach the people, but that they themselves have failed to keep the law.

Priests have become involved in Baal worship and this has allowed, even encouraged, all the people to prostitute themselves. Baal worship involved cultic prostitution—enacting, through fertility rites, the agricultural fecundity that they wanted. In our sensitivity to feminist issues, it is worth noting that Hosea excuses the women and holds only the men accountable (v. 14).

Whether we should attribute the reference to the two southern tribes of Judah (v. 15) to a 'Judean' editor, rather than regarding it as original to Hosea, is a debated point. On either reading, the implication is that Hosea's message has significance beyond its immediate audience. We do well, therefore, not to ignore its challenge to ourselves.

5 Where the judgement falls

Hosea 5

This note will concentrate on verses 1–2 only, as there is more than enough here to occupy us. First we recognise the careful structure. In verse 1a, three groups are addressed directly: priests, the house of Israel and the house of the king. This list concludes with a statement explaining why they have been summoned to give account of themselves before the divine judge. Verses 1b–2 are similar in structure in that there are three places mentioned—Mizpah, Tabor and Shittim—finishing with another judgement statement. However, note also the repeated 'for' statements in verse 1, which suggest a chiastic structure for the two verses.

Moving beyond this formal analysis, there is much to note in the details. In verse 1, the words 'priests' and 'house of the king' indicate groups who were in positions of power and, therefore, especial account-ability to God. This makes the reference to 'house of Israel', which normally refers to all of the ten northern tribes, seem strange. Is Hosea focusing the divine judgement, at one and the same time, on the leaders and the whole populace? It could be his way (and, through him, God's way) of saying to a wider audience, 'The fact that the leaders are especially accountable does not mean that you are not all involved: you will all experience the punishment.' More likely, however, is the view that 'house of Israel' means something like 'elders' in this context. This understand-ing is strengthened if 'For the judgement pertains to you' is understood not to mean initially that God's condemnation is going to fall on them, but rather that the responsibility for upholding justice throughout the tribes is their responsibility. One way or another, this is their role and so

God summons them to 'hear', to pay attention in the lawsuit.

With regard to the three places named, there are disputes about exactly which places are meant, but J.L. Mays tells us that 'each contained a shrine which… had close connections with the worship of Baal' (*Hosea*, p. 81). The criticism of Israel's leaders is not only that they have been involved with these places, but also that they have been responsible for causing the downfall of others through them. Thus three different images for entrapment are used—a snare, a net and a pit.

6 Cheap grace

Hosea 6

It was Dietrich Bonhoeffer, the great German theologian who was executed at the end of World War II, who coined the phrase 'cheap grace', but Hosea describes it vividly in verses 1–3. Whereas older interpreters heard in these words Israel's contrition—and, in the phrase 'on the third day he will raise us up', even a prophecy of the resurrection of Jesus— more probably we should recognise them as Hosea's ironic comment on the people's contrition. They think it is an easy matter to repent, to ensure that God treats them graciously according to his covenant promises. But, as Hosea indicated earlier, 'Their deeds do not permit them to return to their God. For the spirit of whoredom is within them, and they do not know the Lord' (5:4).

So where is the irony? Well, in verse 3, the grounds of their 'security' echo the fertility cults. They cannot escape from the mentality to which they have sold their souls. They think God is bound by the seasons of nature to respond to them. They imagine themselves to be the crops that are fertilised by the spring rains, just as, in the fertility rites, they present themselves as the earth being fertilised by the gods.

Hence God's stinging rebuke. He has slaughtered them by the prophets (v. 5). Maybe this is an echo of the slaughter on Mount Horeb, instigated by Elijah (1 Kings 18:40), but the parallel line suggests not: rather, we should understand the role of prophecy as bringing the judgement of God, through the historical process.

Even so, God's heart is revealed as compassionate and not vindictive.

His plea in verse 4 is, 'What shall I do with you, O Ephraim?' He is at his wits' end, wanting to see Ephraim truly return to him, but formal sacrificial rituals will no longer achieve the true cleansing and restoration that God longs for. Once the worshipper's heart is infested with pagan distortions, the normal procedures for maintaining the covenant lose their efficacy (v. 6).

Judah saw the true cost of unfaithfulness in Israel's destruction by Assyria. Now the message is drilled home for her and for all who read God's word after her (vv. 4b, 11).

Guidelines

- Reading through this book, we can see how prophecies that were originally delivered to the ten northern tribes are also applied to Judah. How important is this 'extension of application' for helping us to understand why and how the Old Testament can and should be regarded as part of our Christian scriptures?
- Reread chapters 1—6 and note down aspects of Hosea's message that could be applied to our own situation. Do you want to distinguish between personal, church and national applications? If so, why?
- To what extent do you think nations and cultures become trapped by their own systems and practices (for example, consumerism, capitalism, militarism or sexualisation) as 5:4 suggests was true for Israel? How can the church model a different way of being, as Hosea sought to do through his own marital situation?
- Pray for situations in our society where, in the light of Hosea's message, we are living in disobedience to God's ways.

1 A silly dove

Hosea 7

So far, Hosea's main focus has been moral and religious apostasy, exemplified in Baal worship. The first section of chapter 7 (vv. 1–10) is probably a reiteration of this theme, as verse 4 indicates: 'They are all adulterers.' The cry from God's and Hosea's heart (it is difficult to distinguish them) is in verse 10: 'Yet they do not return to the Lord their God, or seek him, for all this.'

The 'all this' includes their religious apostasy but there is also an indication of another element: 'Foreigners devour his strength' (v. 9). This is probably a reference to the nations surrounding Israel, which were constantly alluring and bullying Israel into military alliances. Hosea sees these alliances as draining Israel's resources and hastening its old age.

As verses 11–16 tell us, Israel is losing not only its strength but also its mind: 'like a dove, silly and without strength' (v. 11). In its attempt to maintain its independence and survive the threat of the superpowers, Egypt and Assyria, Israel is vacillating between them—or perhaps seeking to play one off against the other. We can see something of these 'power plays' in 2 Kings 15:19—17:4, a passage that ends with the story of Israel paying enforced tribute to Assyria and then liaising with Egypt to escape from it. However, what might have appeared as either a military necessity or political astuteness is actually rebellion against God himself (vv. 15–16).

One of the features that make Hosea's prophecy so powerful—even in the English translation—is his intense use of metaphors. This chapter is a good example of it. Sometimes the metaphors are extended over several verses, as is the case with the 'oven' image (vv. 4–7). This image begins by linking the passion of adultery to the heat of an oven—indeed, an overheated and self-sustaining oven (v. 4)—but then moves on to represent a smouldering resentment (v. 6) that leads to the rulers being ousted (v. 7).

Often the metaphors are short, vivid references—such as the dove flitting around with no direction (v. 11). Yet this image, too, is intensified as God's judgement is expressed in terms of catching a bird in the net (v. 12). Then, Israel is described as a 'defective bow' (v. 16). The Israelites were once strong and effective as a weapon of war because God 'strengthened their arms' (v. 15), but now they are utterly useless.

2 The vulture circles

Hosea 8

Here in verse 1 is another of those powerful metaphors. Unlike the dove that flits about in a harmless and almost comic way, the vulture (perhaps some kind of eagle) is circling around, about to swoop on its prey with deadly effect. So God commands someone ('your' is singular, so perhaps it means the prophet) to sound the trumpet. This may be to warn others of the approaching enemy, but it might also be to announce the beginning of a court ruling, for the verse goes on to say, 'They have broken my covenant.'

Outside the Pentateuch, references to 'covenant' are quite rare, and two of them are in Hosea (see also 6:7). The use of the term here may have been prompted partly by the function of covenants as a form of political and military control during the period of Assyrian dominance. As our sense of covenant is often dominated by our awareness of its use in the Bible, particularly the Old Testament, it is worth reminding ourselves of its political connotations.

Covenant is the term for the formal structure of the relationship instituted by Yahweh's election of Israel. Because of the term's provenance in the political practices of international alliances, it casts Israel in the role of a vassal or servant under the suzerainty of Yahweh who assumes responsibility for their security and establishes the claim of his lordship over them. (Mays, p. 116)

At one level, it is another metaphor (Hosea frequently balances references to this political kind of covenant with language from marriage, which was seen as another sort of covenant). However, it is more than a metaphor, for it encapsulates the complex realities of Israel's relationship with God while intensifying the issues involved, because it involves military practice too. Hosea thus reinforces the clash between Israel's religious and political allegiances.

The disjointed cry in verse 2 is covenant language, appealing to God for help in the face of an oppressor. Behind it is the question 'Why doesn't our covenanted God come to our rescue in the face of military [probably Assyrian] oppression?' The rest of the chapter explains why. In their idolatry and their self-constructed, empty worship, as well as in choosing their own kings (usually forbidden in vassal treaties), they have given evidence of their rebellion and so forfeited any rights to God's intervention. Their punishment is declared: 'They shall return to Egypt' (v. 13). Ironically, the Egyptians, the people to whom they have appealed for help, are those from whom, centuries earlier, God rescued them to form them into 'his people'.

3 The truth about the prophet

Hosea 9

This chapter further explores the theme of Egypt. Normally, for Israel, this image would recall their salvation from the land of Egypt, but here the focus turns to punishment. So, in verse 10, God finds Israel 'like grapes in the wilderness'—something wonderful and refreshing, something to be highly treasured—but most of the chapter is about terrible and apparently final judgement. There is a specific reference to Egypt in verse 6, and verse 16 seems to echo the punishment of the Egyptians in the death of their firstborn.

At the heart of the judgement, we gain a glimpse of Hosea's experience in delivering this message: the people cry out, 'The prophet is a fool, the man of the spirit is mad!' (v. 7). Unlike in Amos 7:10–16 or Jeremiah 20:2 and 38:1–7, there is no narrative context for this outcry against the prophet. It is interesting, however, that the criticism is expressed in poetic parallelism. This suggests that it was an example of memorable propaganda issued by Hosea's political or religious opponents. The description 'man of the spirit' indicates that Hosea was, or at least was perceived to be, in the 'charismatic' line of prophecy. It prompts recollections of the account of Saul receiving the Spirit in 1 Samuel 10:10–13. It is also interesting to note that Saul was on his way to Gilgal when this happened (v. 8), while his receiving of the Spirit was associated with Gibeah—and both Gibeah and Gilgal feature in Hosea 9 (vv. 9, 15).

We do not have any accounts of Hosea exhibiting frenzied behaviour like Saul's, but we do have accounts of his marriage, which may have appeared bizarre, so it is not impossible that some of his actions may have prompted this kind of criticism. To label someone as mad or stupid is one way to devalue anything they say!

This is not God's verdict on Hosea, however: 'The prophet is a sentinel for my God over Ephraim' (v. 8). The theme of the prophet as a sentinel, or watchman, appears elsewhere, too (Jeremiah 6:17; Ezekiel 3:17; Isaiah 56:10), but fulfilling this role was deeply painful and incurred intense hostility. Whether this hostility brought physical abuse for Hosea, as it did for Jeremiah (Jeremiah 20:2; 38:6), we do not know, but it probably involved attempts at public humiliation and would have led to a sense of rejection and loneliness. This antagonism is yet further evidence of Israel's rebellion against God.

4 The fruitful vine?

Hosea 10

Unsurprisingly, the vine is a common biblical picture for Israel: it was a familiar feature of Israel's horticultural environment and an important part of the nation's economy. We find the image in the Psalms (80:8–12) and the prophets (Jeremiah 2:21; Isaiah 5:1–7) and, of course, Jesus alludes to it in his parables (see Matthew 21:28–41).

The vine metaphor usually illustrates the criticism that Israel is unfruit-ful and unfaithful and warrants judgement from God. Here in Hosea 10, though, there is a twist: Israel *is* a fruitful vine, but the fruit is 'for himself' (v. 1, NIV). Worse still, the Israelites have 'eaten the fruit of lies' because they have relied on their own resources and resourcefulness (v. 13).

This passage is a serious challenge to anyone tempted by the 'prosper-ity gospel' or anything like it. The fruit increased and the land prospered, but this was a sign neither of faithfulness to God nor of his blessing. Israel responded to her prosperity by building more altars (as, at vari-ous times in English history, successful people have built churches), but these altars were not in honour of Yahweh, the one who found Israel like a vine in the desert and rescued her (9:10). They were altars consecrated to the worship of Baal, the god of fertility—so God's judgement will soon become apparent.

This judgement will not be arbitrary; it will be appropriate. The wor-ship of Baal celebrated the fruitfulness of the land through religious rituals with the king at their centre. So 'Samaria and its king will float away like a twig on the surface of the waters' (v. 7, NIV 1984). Samaria, the imposing capital city, will be destroyed along with its king. What appears to provide stability and security is nothing but 'Pooh sticks'! The altars will be overrun with thistles (v. 8); Bethel, the cult centre for fertility, will be a place of devastation and death (v. 15) and the priests will be discredited.

How daunting it must have been for those left in Judah, after the Assyrian invasion established the veracity of Hosea's words, to read that a similar fate of total servitude awaited them too (see v. 11). And yet, much against the grain of this message, there is hope: 'It is time to seek the Lord, that he may come and rain righteousness on you' (v. 12).

5 Hope against hope

Hosea 11:1—12:10

How can there be any hope? The Israelites have totally broken their covenant with Yahweh. Morally and religiously they have forfeited any right to a future with God. Furthermore, God has pronounced his judgement. Surely Israel's future is a destination already written in stone.

Within the structure of a political or religious covenant, this would be so, but Hosea knows of a more costly covenant—marriage. Even when one partner has totally shattered that covenant, love can remain. Love can be renewed; love cannot be denied—and within a broken marriage the bond between parent and child can survive.

In order to understand and communicate the deepest mystery of God's love for his rebellious and stubborn people, then, Hosea engages with another metaphor from human relationships. So in 11:1, 3–4 we read, 'When Israel was a child, I loved him, and out of Egypt I called my son... It was I who taught Ephraim to walk, I took them up in my arms... I led them with cords of human kindness... I bent down to them and fed them.'

Although this passage is deeply embedded in human love at its most tender, we are never allowed to forget that it is a metaphor for a historical process: there is a reference to Egypt, and 'my son' is followed by the plural pronoun, 'them'. Even more tellingly, these lines are bound together with the story of Israel's rebellion (v. 2). At one level, then, the use of this familial metaphor intensifies Israel's guilt and justifies any punishment. Nevertheless, God says, 'How can I give you up, Ephraim? … My heart is changed within me; all my compassion is aroused' (v. 8, NIV).

The conclusion is reached: 'I will not… destroy Ephraim' (v. 9). Yet that is what happened historically! Here we come face to face with some troubling questions. Have sin and rebellion finally triumphed over God's grace and mercy? Has God's mercy failed in the face of the powers of evil and violence? The story of Jacob may hold some clues (12:1–6). In spite of his duplicity, he did return to God. So God holds out the hope that he will, one day, gather his scattered peoples back (11:9–11).

6 Squaring the circle

Hosea 13:4–14; 14:1–7

God's dilemma is this: Israel (or Ephraim), the northern tribes, have been chosen by God, rescued from Egypt and provided for during the wilderness wanderings (13:4–6). They have been nurtured into nationhood by God's continuing loving attention, expressed through covenant, law, and institutions such as the monarchy, priesthood and the prophets. Yet Israel constantly betrays God and deserves punishment. Worse than this, Israel seems incapable of behaving any differently, so the only thing left to do is to destroy her. But God is wedded to Israel; alternatively, Israel is his child. Either way, his love for and commitment to the nation constantly pull him back from the appropriate step of annihilation (see 11:8–10).

If the whole of Hosea can be viewed as an extended exploration of this dilemma, then 13:14 provides a microcosmic example. 'Shall I ransom them from the power of Sheol? Shall I redeem them from Death?' Do these questions summarise God's self-questioning, as if he can't quite make up his mind? Or do they anticipate the answer 'Surely not'? The fact that Sheol was often considered to be just beyond God's jurisdiction (see Isaiah 28:18; Psalm 6:5; 30:9) simply highlights the enigma. If God does not rescue them from Sheol, is it because he cannot or because he chooses not to? To add further to the puzzle, these sentences can legitimately be read as assertions: 'I will deliver this people from the power of the grave…' (NIV).

The same ambivalence continues to the end of verse 14: the word translated in the NRSV as 'compassion' occurs only here in the Hebrew Bible, and it could also be translated 'vengeance'. So is it compassion or vengeance that Yahweh refuses to contemplate?

Paul, of course, opts for a positive reading in 1 Corinthians 15:55, but he does this not only on the basis of the Greek translation of the Old Testament but also in the light of the resurrection of Jesus and the anticipation of the second coming. This helps us perceive why, within Hosea's messages and, indeed, the whole of the Old Testament, the dilemma experienced by Hosea in his marital relationship and explored in his prophetic oracles was not resolved. It needed the creative intervention by God in Christ. For this, Hosea could only wait and we can only worship.

Guidelines

Some of the many enriching features of this book are the ways that Hosea (a) reflects deeply about the traditions of his faith, including the exodus and wilderness wanderings, even the patriarchal stories, (b) is aware of contemporary events both within and beyond Israel, and (c) expresses his message in vivid, fresh and powerful metaphors.

Reflect on the implications of this for the task of communicating the Christian faith in our world today. If it helps, choose a specific issue (for example, capitalism, ecology or sexualisation) and think through a Christian response using the three points above.

Pray for all involved in this demanding but invigorating challenge, such as film makers, musicians, journalists, politicians (including local councillors), parents, teachers, youth workers and preachers.

How can we help people who, perhaps with their children or their partner, have to cope with continuing unfaithfulness, betrayal and deep pain? Does Hosea's experience suggest that we need to be willing to share their suffering ourselves? Are there ways in which your church community is doing this?

FURTHER READING
James Luther Mays, Hosea, SCM, 1969.
Douglas Stuart, Hosea–Jonah (Word Biblical Commentary), Thomas Nelson, 1987.

Acts 1:1—8:25

Acts alone in the New Testament tells of Jesus' followers after his resurrection. It has the same author as Luke's Gospel (Luke 1:1–4; Acts 1:1). Luke aims to tell his patron Theophilus about the growth of the earliest believing communities in the 40 years after Jesus' resurrection.

The earliest believers were Jewish, and Acts is soaked in Old Testament scripture, for Luke wants his readers to realise that the church is not a new thing. It isn't God's 'plan B' after his 'plan A' (choosing Israel) failed. Rather, there is continuity between what God has been doing long into Israel's history and what God is now doing. So Luke regularly points to scriptural passages to interpret events in the church's beginning, growth and establishment around the Mediterranean basin, starting in Jerusalem (1:8).

For Luke, then, a major concern of his story is the restoration of Israel. The Old Testament prophets looked forward to a time when God would restore his people's fortunes. During the Babylonian exile of the sixth century BC, they longed for a 'new exodus' that would take them out of Babylon, a thousand miles from home, to their own land. But although the people returned under Ezra and Nehemiah's leadership and although the temple was rebuilt, many of these prophecies were still unfulfilled, so people of Jesus' day looked forward to God accomplishing this 'new exodus' in full.

Luke 3:4–6 places Isaiah 40:3–5 prominently at the start of John the baptiser's ministry. Isaiah portrays the return from exile as a journey on a highway direct from Babylon to Israel, across the arid, mountainous desert, and Luke understands the baptiser's role as preparing the way for Jesus himself ('the salvation of God', Luke 3:6) to come. As Acts begins, the disciples are hoping for Israel's promised restoration, and they ask the risen Jesus when it will be (1:6). Jewish people expected Israel's restoration to involve ruling over the nations (see, for example, Isaiah 60:12; Zechariah 8:20–23), but scripture also spoke of the other nations being blessed through Israel at the time of restoration (Isaiah 49:6, echoed in Acts 1:8, quoted in Acts 13:47). Acts is the story of Israel's restoration in a way that embraces and includes the nations. Read on!

Quotations are taken from the New International Version of the Bible.

1 Jesus' mission, continued

Acts 1:1–11

Losing someone you love is a terrible shock, and Jesus' followers face a second bereavement. The Lord they love died, but came back! Now he is leaving again, and will no longer be physically present. Here Jesus prepares them for this future.

Luke notes that Jesus will not stop working after he ascends to heaven, for this book of Acts is about what Jesus will *continue* to do and teach (compare v. 1). How will this happen?

First, Jesus teaches and equips the apostles in a 40-day seminar (vv. 2–5); much of their later speaking will be rooted in what they learn of how to read scripture (what we call the Old Testament) through a 'Jesus' lens during this time. We shall see the impact of this learning in Peter's Pentecost speech (2:14–36), where he reads key Old Testament passages as speaking about Jesus.

Second, Jesus is still in the business of restoring Israel to what it was meant to be. However, Israel will not rule the other nations, as many expected (perhaps including the apostles, v. 6): rather, Israel will *embrace and include* other nations, 'to the ends of the earth' (v. 8). The Old Testament vision of passages such as Zechariah 8:20–23, which portray the nations coming to Jerusalem, will be expanded, as the believers go from Jerusalem to the nations. The timing of this process is hidden from people—only the Father knows (v. 7)—but it is certain, and it will bring Jesus to earth again (v. 11).

Meanwhile, the apostles are to participate in Jesus' restoration mission when empowered by the Spirit. They will be Jesus' ambassadors ('witnesses', v. 8), sent by him to represent him and to speak for him to many people. During this time of mission (which still goes on today), Jesus will be present among them by the Spirit, enabling them to do what they could not do alone. The Spirit is God's power and presence. Their Spirit-empowered testimony will bring others to a right verdict on Jesus, a verdict that reverses the mistaken human verdict of crucifixion.

Third, Jesus will not be absent from the scene; he is now in heaven, alongside the Father (v. 11). Jesus is in the place of power and authority in the universe, and acts from there to strengthen and equip his followers for his mission (see 9:3–6, 10–16, 34).

2 The Spirit launches the mission

Acts 2:1–13

An extraordinary sound-and-vision experience is the public launch of the believers' mission 'to the ends of the earth' (1:8). Key divine promises are fulfilled as the Spirit falls on Jesus' followers and enables them to speak in other languages (2:4).

There are echoes of Old Testament scripture here, for Pentecost was a celebration of the time when God gave the law to Moses on Mount Sinai. The loud noise, the experience of God's presence (here, by the Spirit) and the beginning of a new period of redemptive history are all key echoes (see Exodus 19:16–19; 24:17). By contrast, while Moses' experience centred on God's gift of the law, this experience centres on Jesus' gift of the Spirit: the Spirit will do for the new covenant people of God what the law was intended to do for the old covenant people. As Jeremiah (31:31–34) and Ezekiel (36:26–27) prophesied, the Spirit empowers people to live God's way from the inside out, by contrast with the law, which worked only from the outside in. Peter's transformation, from a man who three times denied Jesus (Luke 22:54–62) to one who now speaks boldly for Jesus, is a striking example of the Spirit's transforming power at work.

Not only is scripture being fulfilled but so are Jesus' promises (1:5, 8). The fire echoes John the baptiser's promise (Luke 3:16) and shows that Jesus' disciples are now cleansed by the Spirit's fire and fit for the task of witness.

The crowd's reactions show that the phenomena were public, visible and audible. Probably, the initial event (vv. 1–4) took place in the upstairs room where the believers met (1:13), and the believers (at least the Twelve, v. 14) then went out onto the streets. Jerusalem had wide avenues, and they might have gone into the large temple courts, where a large crowd could gather.

The crowd is divided, as will frequently happen throughout Acts in reaction to gospel proclamation (see 13:42–45): many express puzzled wonder (vv. 6–7, 12), while some are scornful (v. 13). We should not be surprised today when people reject or scorn the gospel message or the actions of Jesus' followers: nothing is new. In such situations we are called, like Peter (2:14–36), to explain what is happening, testify to Jesus and leave the results in God's hands.

3 Peter testifies to Jesus and invites response

Acts 2:14–36

Peter responds to the crowd's divided reaction by explaining the phenomena they are experiencing. His explanation is rooted in scripture and is a vehicle for telling the story of Jesus, including his death and resurrection and his exaltation to the Father's right hand. Peter's speech aims to change hearts, and his testimony here focuses on Jesus in order to achieve that aim. It is hard to show the full extent of this focus in English, but the original language highlights words by locating them at the start of sentences and clauses: 'Jesus of Nazareth… this man… this man… this Jesus… this Jesus' (vv. 22–24, 32, 36).

While the focus of the speech is Jesus, God is the subject of most of the verbs: Peter's speech is about what *God* has done in and through Jesus. God acted through Jesus' ministry (v. 22). God's purposes were accomplished in Jesus' death at the hands of the people of Jerusalem and their leaders (v. 23). God raised Jesus from death (v. 24). God spoke in scripture to announce these events (vv. 25–31, 34–35, quoting Psalms 16:8–11a; 110:1). Most significantly, God exalted Jesus to the position of authority at his right hand and gave Jesus the Spirit to pour out (v. 33). God's actions in Jesus persuade the audience of their responsibility for Jesus' death ('*you*… put him to death', v. 23: see the response, v. 37) and call them to give Jesus the honour he rightly deserves (v. 36).

The Christian movement is a Jesus movement, a God movement and a Spirit movement. Recognising Jesus as the one who now gives the Spirit (v. 33) places Jesus in the same category as Yahweh, the God of Israel, because in the Old Testament and in later Jewish writings it is Yahweh and Yahweh alone who can give the Spirit. This full-orbed portrait of God leads to the Christian understanding of God as Trinity: believers are invited to share in the life of this triune God.

Peter's speech invites us to reflect on the way we communicate our faith to others, as individuals and as Christian communities. Like Peter, we need to keep our focus on Jesus, speak clearly of God and combine our testimony of who Jesus is with testimony of what he has done, both in the early days of the Christian movement and today.

4 Models of response to the gospel

Acts 2:37–47; 4:32–37

The gospel is wonderful good news: it tells us of God's transforming love through Jesus and by the Spirit. The gospel offer is total: God accepts us without reservation through Jesus. The gospel demand is total, too: God engages with every part of our lives. These two passages portray how to receive what the gospel offers. Responding to the gospel involves five key elements (2:38–39), which recur throughout Acts where people come to faith.

'Repent' means to change one's mind: Peter's hearers had to change their minds about Jesus, because they were complicit in his crucifixion (v. 23). People today vitally need a similar change, from a low view of Jesus to a high one, and from a high view of themselves ('I can manage without God') to a low one ('I am nothing without God'). 'Be baptised' is passive, for people do not baptise themselves: they receive baptism, symbolising that they receive God's gift in Jesus.

These two elements have three consequences. First, people are forgiven their sins: God wipes the slate clean and a new relationship with God is opened up. Second, believers receive the Spirit as a gift from God, and the Spirit makes the presence of Jesus real and personal, as well as empowering us to live for Jesus. Third, believers become part of a community formed by God: 'all whom the Lord our God will call' (v. 39)— and therein is a great challenge.

Christian community involves shared life. The earliest believers met daily (2:46) and learned together from the apostles (v. 42): these were days long before the writing of the New Testament scriptures, so the Twelve formed a vital living source for the stories of Jesus (see 1:21–22). When we listen together to the apostolic testimony of the New Testament, we join the early believers in devoting ourselves 'to the apostles' teaching'.

The sharing goes beyond meeting to eating. Acts 2:46 suggests that eating together happened both in homes and in the larger meetings in the temple, which would have had an evangelistic impact on not-yet-believers (2:47; 4:33). Their sharing was remarkable: people were ready and willing to sell things to help believers in need (2:44–45; 4:32–37). The change that Jesus brought to them was so deep that their money and possessions were held lightly, as God's gifts to be shared. In such a community, it is no surprise that God did remarkable 'wonders and signs' (2:43; see 4:33).

5 Jesus heals today

Acts 3:1–10

Prayer, wonders and signs, and the temple have been important themes in Acts so far, and these three come together in this remarkable story of healing, which initiates a sequence of events running through to 4:31.

Peter and John approach the temple to pray at the time of the afternoon sacrifice, 3.00 pm (v. 1). Here is a signal that, at this time, the believing community was not separate from Judaism but was a renewal movement within it. Through the believers, Jesus' restoration of Israel was taking place (1:6–8).

The man with a congenital disability of the legs was excluded from participation in temple worship and sacrifice (see 2 Samuel 5:8; Deuteronomy 23:1; Leviticus 21:18–20). Not only that, but he was economically dependent on others, mainly his family, for he could not work. Helping such people was commended (Job 29:15), so people with disabilities gathered at the temple entrances to invite gifts from visitors. Isaiah looked forward to the day when lame people would be able to 'leap like a deer' (35:6; see also Micah 4:6–7)—and this was that day for this man!

Somehow Peter and John knew that Jesus would heal the lame man that day (vv. 4, 6). Jesus acted from heaven through Peter to bring physical restoration to him, as his lower limbs became strong (v. 7). The first place the healed man went was the very place from which he had been excluded for his whole life—the temple courts (v. 8). He entered with utter joy, jumping and giving God praise, for not only was he physically well but he could now work, become economically productive, find a wife and join in with community life. He is the restoration of Israel in miniature.

The restoration of Israel is inclusive of those who have been excluded: this man is a remarkable example, but many more will follow. The multi-ethnic crowd at Pentecost (2:9–11) foreshadows the inclusion of people from many races and nations in the restored Israel; this man's experience foreshadows the inclusion of Jewish people who were previously excluded. We can hear an echo of Jesus' healings in Luke's Gospel, such as that of the woman who bled profusely (Luke 8:43–48): Jesus called her forward so that everyone knew that she had been restored to the community of Israel (see also Luke 13:10–17).

6 Testifying to Jesus' healing power

Acts 3:11–26

The early believers' lives raised questions for those around them, and these questions opened the door for the believers to speak about Jesus. The healing of the man at the Beautiful Gate (3:1–10) gives Peter the opportunity to speak to the people in the temple about Jesus, and he does so in similar terms to the Pentecost speech (2:14–36), although the starting point here is different.

Peter again focuses on Jesus; his key concern is that his hearers' understanding of Jesus might be reversed. They participated in calling for his death (vv. 13–15), and Peter testifies that Jesus is now alive (v. 16) and available to forgive their sins (v. 19). Jesus' resurrection is the key event that shows who he is and what he does—that he is 'the author of life', the one who originates life itself (v. 15). Remarkably for a first-century Jew who believed that there was only one true God, Peter treats Jesus as the proper object of faith whose name is powerful (v. 16). The early Christians did not baldly say, 'Jesus is God', for people in their world believed in many gods. The first question is who God is, and Peter's answer is that God is the God of Israel (v. 13), known in the past through scripture (vv. 18, 21–22) and now in Jesus. This God offers a way back to knowledge of him (v. 19).

This is good news not only for the present but also for the future: Jesus will return at the end, when God restores everything to its rightful place and state (v. 21). In the meantime, believers experience 'times of refreshing' (v. 19): the life of the age to come breaks into this age so that people experience its power, as the healed man has done. The healing of the man is one example of this 'refreshing', as is the generous sharing of possessions among the believing community.

All of this requires a response: Peter calls the people to repent (v. 19), to change their understanding and redirect their lives. If all of his testimony is true, the people of God is being redefined around Jesus, and to reject him is to lose your place among God's people (v. 23).

Guidelines

How transformed are we? These opening chapters describe a 'big bang': God does remarkable things and people are transformed over a relatively short period. The 120 believers (1:15) are galvanised and changed by the Spirit's coming, being enabled to witness boldly to Jesus. Peter, who three times denied he knew Jesus, now speaks with great power, at Pentecost, in the temple courts, and even before the authorities. The community grows as 3000, and then more than 5000, respond to the gospel.

Such growth brought its challenges, and the readiness of believers to sell their possessions to provide for others in need was vital to the community's life. The rubber hit the road here: Christian life and experience was not just warm and fuzzy feelings, but touched people's bank balances and led them to give to others as generously as God had given to them in Jesus Christ (see 2 Corinthians 8:9).

It's worth reflecting, particularly for those of us who live in the affluent West, on how far our Christian commitment affects our use of money and possessions. A study in Britain some years ago suggested that Christians' spending patterns were similar to those of their non-believing contemporaries, with one difference: what Christians gave to church and mission was similar to what non-believers spent on alcohol and tobacco. The British situation has changed, of course; nevertheless, this raises the question of whether we Christians simply buy into our culture's attitudes concerning money and possessions, rather than having values and attitudes shaped by the gospel.

Reflect on your spending. Try keeping a record for three months of what you spend, so that you have a clear picture. Some outgoings will be fixed (for example, taxes, rent/mortgage and food), so focus on the more flexible spending (the amount will vary from person to person considerably), and consider and pray about whether you want to use this money differently. The key issue is not the amount but the generosity of heart you show (2 Corinthians 8:12). Might you want to give more to Christian work and mission, or contribute to others in need, or make a gift to a Christian minister or worker to help them to have a holiday? Be creative and imaginative as you pray about this issue.

1 Who speaks for God?

Acts 4:1–22

Asking who speaks for God is a big issue today, just as it was a big question in the days of the earliest Christians. This story presents a sharp division between two sets of people who claim to speak for God—the Jewish authorities and the apostles.

The Jewish authorities were the Sanhedrin, the ruling council of the Jewish people. They believed that their reading of scripture was right: they had found Jesus guilty of blasphemy (Luke 22:66—23:2), and so, they thought, his followers could not be speaking truly for God. But they were wrong, and their failure challenges us in our lives as people who seek to speak and live for God. Might we be in the same danger, in spite of our claims?

Luke signals that the Sanhedrin are wrong by narrating God's empowering of Peter by the Spirit (v. 8), which produces surprising boldness and cogency (v. 13). Peter focuses on God's attestation of Jesus in raising Jesus from the dead (v. 10, echoing 2:36). This is why Jesus' name is powerful in healing and bringing a bigger salvation (v. 12).

The Sanhedrin, by contrast, do not even speak of God. They are concerned only with how they can suppress this new movement, in spite of the incontrovertible evidence of the lame man's healing (vv. 14–18). They may be an example of 'blasphemy against the Holy Spirit' (Luke 12:10), for they refuse to listen to the Spirit-inspired apostolic testimony.

Peter and John courageously stand for Jesus, refusing to be cowed by threats: the only question they are interested in is about what God wants (vv. 19–20). When challenged in this way, the Sanhedrin are powerless, for, again, they cannot argue with the evidence of the man's healing (vv. 21–22): they can only bluster and threaten.

To speak for God-known-in-Jesus among those who are not (yet) Christian believers is both a great privilege and a great challenge. At times it requires confronting the false claims of not-yet-believers, as here, and it can involve threats and suffering. Yet, like Peter and John, we need to live our lives before an 'audience of one'—God himself, known in Jesus by the Spirit—and ask what God wants from us.

2 The Christians' vital breath

Acts 4:23–31

You learn what matters most to someone by listening to them pray. This shows what is really on their mind and heart. Here the believers face pressure, and it drives them to prayer—a contrast with their failure in the garden of Gethsemane (Luke 22:39–46). There, Jesus called them to pray and they failed; now, facing a great challenge, they turn to prayer. The lesson has been learned and embedded in them by the Spirit's coming. This is the only prayer recorded in Acts, so how do the believers pray in response to the authorities' threats (vv. 17, 21)?

This prayer focuses on God and what God does: God is the sovereign ruler of the universe. The first word of the prayer addresses God as 'Sovereign Lord' (v. 24), translating a rare word that speaks of the absolute rule of a person. The Greek Old Testament uses this word four times when

Daniel prays in difficult circumstances (Daniel 9:8, 15, 16, 17). Not only does God rule, but God's sovereign power is seen in his creation (v. 24), his revelation of himself in the words of scripture (vv. 25–26, quoting Psalm 2:1–2), and in his plan, which is seen and realised in and through the trial, death and resurrection of Jesus (v. 28). Human attempts to frustrate God's purposes fail: rulers may try, but their efforts are futile because God will checkmate them (vv. 27–28).

The believers draw on David's words in Psalm 2 to encourage each other and to interpret their present experience: here is another example of 'this is what was spoken' by Old Testament saints (see 2:16). Reading our experience through the lens of scripture will bring clarity and focus, for it will show us clearly what is most important, where our responsibility lies, and where our responsibility ends and God's begins.

Thus the believers ask God to move and act, not to rescue them from the difficult situation but to enable them to continue to speak for Jesus (v. 29) and to perform 'signs and wonders' that they cannot do (v. 30). Threats and suffering do not cause them to be cowed into silence and acquiescence with the authorities' desires. Rather, they know they can face those threats only with God's power and equipping—and it comes (v. 31).

3 Putting God before human authorities

Acts 5:12–42

There are times when God's work is almost pure comedy, and this is one of those times. The guards are embarrassed not only because they have to report that their prisoners are missing, but also because they are then told that the prisoners are now in a public place—the temple—doing exactly what caused their arrest in the first place (vv. 22–25). Imagine the irritation among the jealous Sanhedrin (v. 17), who have assembled to deal with the apostles (v. 21b)!

As earlier, so here: God is the one driving the mission forward. Human authorities may seek to suppress testimony to Jesus but God acts so that people can hear and receive the gospel message. God frees his witnesses from prison (vv. 17–26), the apostles rightly assert that answering to God is far more important than answering to human authorities (vv. 27–33; see 4:18–20), and God enables his witnesses to go on speaking to that end (vv. 34–42).

Gamaliel's intervention (vv. 34–39), as a loyal Sanhedrin member, is striking. We know of him as a highly regarded teacher from later Jewish writings (the Mishnah): he taught Saul of Tarsus (Acts 22:3). There is great irony in the advice of this Sanhedrin member—from a group that opposes the believers—on how not to oppose God's will (vv. 38–39). Gamaliel shares the Pharisaic belief in resurrection from the dead, and yet the Pharisees in the Sanhedrin reject the apostles' testimony to Jesus' resurrection (vv. 30–32), thus echoing the lack of spiritual perception they show in Luke's Gospel (see Luke 7:30). While Gamaliel's speech prevents the Sanhedrin from stoning the apostles (at least for now), it does not prevent them from publicly shaming the apostles by beating them (vv. 40–41).

To respond rightly to the apostles' testimony would have involved humility on the part of the Sanhedrin, for they would have had to admit that they were deeply wrong and then publicly stand up and say so by being baptised. To become a Christian today is a similar process, and we need to beware making it too easy and avoiding the humiliation that is a necessary part of repentance—admitting we are wrong. To live as a Christian involves a continuing humility of this kind, too, for we continue to be wrong and need to keep turning to God for forgiveness day by day.

4 Dealing with conflict

Acts 6:1–7

Church life is rarely free of conflict, whether about music, style of worship, preaching, organisation or other things. We might have thought there was little conflict in the early believing community (other than in 5:1–11), and could wonder why life was so idyllic then. But here it comes!

The conflict centres on provision for widows—a needy group, for they lacked a family to support them. In Scripture, care for widows is a key index of faithfulness to God, since it shows that people share God's compassion (for example, Deuteronomy 10:18; 24:17–21). The believers are a mix of Aramaic-speakers ('Hebraic Jews') and Greek-speakers ('Hellenistic Jews'). The former are native Palestinian Jews, and the latter are Jews from elsewhere (the 'Diaspora') who have relocated to Palestine. The Hellenistic Jews think their widows are not being treated fairly in the financial and food provision made for widows (v. 1), so a dispute arises and the apostles are rapidly brought into the picture (v. 2).

The apostles do not, however, seek to resolve the dispute themselves: their focus is on teaching and prayer (vv. 2, 4). It's not that they are avoiding getting their hands dirty by serving in the kitchen: it's about ensuring that their teaching and evangelistic ministry is not neglected, for the church depends on it (2:42; 4:33; 5:14).

The Twelve initiate a community process to resolve matters (v. 2). The whole church takes responsibility for this issue, since it is important to embody what they believe about God's care and compassion for the needy. The community choose seven—all with Greek names, so they may well have been Hellenistic Jews (v. 5). Despite the NIV's translation ('They presented them to the apostles, *who* prayed...'), the most natural reading of the Greek in verse 6 is that 'they'—the whole community—both present the seven to the apostles *and* lay hands on them. The whole community commissions the seven for the task by prayer and laying hands on them.

The church continues to grow (v. 7), not simply because of well-fed widows but because the care for the widows shows the reality of the community's faith, and the appointment of the seven frees the Twelve to continue focusing on prayer, evangelism and teaching.

5 Stephen: administrator and evangelist

Acts 6:8—7:8; 7:44—8:1a

We easily put people in boxes: they're good with the kids or at catering or caring for people having a tough time, and so on. People can then be trapped into the same area of church life for years, so that they become stale in the task and others can't get involved. Being open to God's gifting of people in new areas is a key attitude of good leaders and good congregations, and Stephen models such a change.

Stephen is one of the seven chosen to care for the Hellenistic widows (6:5), and now he shows up as an evangelist and defender of the gospel who argues successfully (vv. 9–10), does remarkable things (v. 8) and looks amazing (v. 15). If there was opposition in the church to Stephen's actions as an evangelist, we don't read about it.

Inevitably, Stephen's ministry attracts opposition (vv. 9, 11–14), and he is hauled up before the Jewish authorities (v. 12). Stephen's speech in 7:2–56 (the longest single speech in Acts) responds to the charges, not by answering point by point (the opposition were telling lies, in any case, 6:13–14), but by showing that God is not tied to particular places.

Stephen argues that the temple, so highly valued by the people, is coming to its sell-by date: it was great in its time (7:44–47), but now Jesus is taking the temple's role of mediation between God and people. So it is a mistake to think, as some do, that God lives in the temple (vv. 48–50). God always worked outside the temple and the land of Israel: he appeared to Abraham in Mesopotamia (vv. 2–3); he went with Joseph to Egypt (vv. 9–15); he stood with Moses in Egypt (vv. 20–22) and appeared to him in the Sinai desert (vv. 30–34).

Stephen's speech climaxes with his accusation that the Sanhedrin are like their ancestors: they do not listen to God, and they resist God (v. 51). This is too much, and they stone him to death—the death prescribed for those who abandon Yahweh (Leviticus 20:2). Stephen prays to Jesus as they attack him (v. 59). Here is clear evidence that the believers were putting Jesus in the same category as Yahweh, and so the stoners were right that Stephen was undermining their beliefs.

As Stephen dies, however, a young man is watching, minding the stoners' cloaks (7:58; 8:1). We shall hear much more of him later!

6 Persecution and growth: inseparable twins

Acts 8:1b–25

During the communist revolution of the 1950s, China threw out Christian missionaries. Western Christians feared that this would be the end of Christianity in that country. But when China began to open up to the rest of the world some 30 years later, the churches had grown, even during the cultural revolution of the 1960s, when religion was banned in China. Today there are more Chinese Christians than ever, and today's growth is rooted in the persecution during that difficult period.

Persecution is a key driver of the earliest church's growth, too. The Jewish authorities attack the believers and seek to imprison them, led by Saul (vv. 1, 3). The result is that these (largely anonymous) believers are scattered to other places, such as Damascus in the north (9:1–2), Joppa on the coast (9:36, 43), and Antioch in Syria, the coastal region of Phoenicia, and Cyprus (11:19–20). As they go, they speak of Jesus to the people they meet—and the church grows (v. 4).

Philip is one of the few travelling believers whose names we know. Like Stephen, he was one of the seven (6:5), and he travels to Samaria. There was a historic divide between Judeans and Samaritans: the Samaritans were considered half-breed heretics who only accepted the first five books of the Old Testament and had their own temple (John 4:20). Yet Philip does not hesitate to speak of Jesus as Messiah there (v. 5). Thus, a major racial barrier is overcome *through persecution*, without which the believers would not have gone to Samaria.

Great signs are performed (vv. 6–8), but the gospel meets a challenge in the shape of Simon the sorcerer (vv. 9–11). Simon is baptised (v. 13) but hasn't fully understood how generous God is: when Peter and John come and pray for the Spirit to come on the Samaritan believers, he wants to buy the power to do the same (vv. 18–19). He doesn't understand that God's Spirit is a free gift, and Peter calls him to change his attitude (vv. 21–23). Simon's response seems open, and the fact that he is not struck down, as Ananias and Sapphira were (5:5, 10), suggests that he may have gone on to repent of his error.

Guidelines

The thread of suffering runs deeply through the Christian life. Jesus told his followers to expect suffering, mirroring and echoing his own suffering (Luke 21:12; John 15:20). In parts of the world today where faith is unwelcome or actively hated, suffering is a daily reality for Christians. Even in the comfortable West, there are signs that Christian faith is unwelcome in the public square and is becoming marginalised and privatised.

In Acts 4—8, believers often encounter suffering for their allegiance to Jesus, and their response is to pray and continue to live faithfully as God calls them to live, testifying to Jesus. They do this so clearly that others are deeply impressed, even though some hesitate to join them (5:13). Luke does not describe them praying that the persecution will stop: their concern is much more about being faithful during persecution, knowing the promise of Jesus that the Spirit will give them words to say (Luke 12:11–12).

These stories invite us to pray with confidence for fellow Christians who suffer for their faith in Jesus—that they will be sustained in their faith and will continue to live with integrity and love; that their testimony to Jesus will be clear and winsome; that God will do remarkable things and that, through their testimony, others will come to faith.

Visit the Christian Solidarity Worldwide website (www.csw.org.uk), read about countries where Christians suffer, and pray for such believers. If you belong to a small group in your church, consider 'adopting' a particular country that your group can pray for regularly.

These stories also call us to reflect on our situation, considering where there are threats to our church's witness to Jesus. What are the threats for your church in your community? We are reminded not to be surprised when we face opposition, even if it is not 'in your face' in the way that it was for these believers in Acts or for many believers today. Acts also offers us models of how to respond, both in encountering those who oppose our faith and mission and in praying for God to continue to act through us and in support of our testimony to Jesus.

FURTHER READING

Beverly R. Gaventa, *Acts* (Abingdon NT Commentary), Abingdon Press, 2003.
Tom Wright, *Acts for Everyone* (two volumes), SPCK, 2008.

The kingdom of God

The central message of Jesus and the focus of his life was 'the kingdom of God'. Matthew, Mark and Luke mention it around 100 times between them, overlapping hugely in what they record but with distinctive emphases, too. Most obviously, Matthew refers to the kingdom 'of heaven' rather than 'of God', but he means the same thing. John only mentions the kingdom a couple of times, favouring the idea of 'eternal life', which is similar. The rest of the New Testament mentions it less, focusing on the proclamation of Jesus as King or Lord rather than 'the kingdom', although the kingdom still underlies its theology.

The idea of the kingdom of God is complex and fluid, and it is not easy to fit everything that is said about it neatly together. Over the years, people have interpreted the idea in many different ways, some stressing its present dimension and ignoring the future, while others see it exclusively as apocalyptic. However we interpret individual passages, the kingdom is both present and future. It was inaugurated in Jesus' mission and will be completed at his return. We live in the overlap of two ages, since the kingdom is already here but is not yet fully consummated.

The Gospels always emphasise that the kingdom is the kingdom *of God*. God is the prime mover and sovereign ruler in this kingdom. So we should never hijack the concept to serve our own particular agendas, however good they are—whether of social reform or charismatic experience, world evangelisation or secular politics, humanitarian good or inner spirituality. The kingdom is about God reclaiming his rule in the world, in surprising and unexpected ways, through his Son, Jesus the Messiah.

Much teaching about the kingdom occurs in the parables, some of which we will examine next week. Far from being transparent stories, easily understood, their meaning was often subversive, undermining conventional thought and hard to grasp, as the disciples' reactions show.

Quotations are taken from the New International Version of the Bible.

1 The revolution begins

Mark 1:14–15

Jesus launched his public ministry saying, 'The time has come. The kingdom of God has come near. Repent and believe the good news!' Packed with meaning, these few words sum up the purpose of his coming and the substance of his message.

Israel had always believed that God was their king, at least in theory. Their behaviour often suggested that they weren't willing to be ruled by him and their experience often left them doubting his power. If God was king, as the prophets and psalmists claimed, why had the nation experienced such political misfortune and, by Jesus' day, fallen under Roman military occupation? Simeon, like many others, was 'waiting for the consolation of Israel' (Luke 2:25), and Joseph from Arimathea was 'waiting for the kingdom of God' (23:51). They longed for the day when God would transparently resume his rightful rule over his people and bring them freedom. Jesus' first words in Mark's Gospel announced that that time was now.

The word 'kingdom' can mislead us. We use it to refer to a territory but, in this case, it is a dynamic word, referring to God's active rulership. Jesus claimed that God was taking over his world again and re-establishing his authority. People thought their problem was that the Romans had usurped God's authority, but the truth was more complex. All sorts of alien powers had invaded God's world and were controlling their lives, as Mark's Gospel records. They included demons, death and disease, sin and injustice, and even well-meaning religious authorities who got in the way of God. Behind them all was Satan, the strong man who needed to be taken prisoner (Mark 3:23–27).

Although Jesus may mean 'the kingdom is approaching', he almost certainly means that, with his coming, 'the kingdom has arrived'. His original audience struggled to understand this because of the surprising nature of the revolution. Jesus turned their expectations upside down: his revolution led him to conquer not with armies and battles, but by a life of love, an unjust death and a powerful resurrection. In Jesus, God's revolution was taking hold.

Jesus summons people to join him in the revolution. That's what 'repenting' and 'believing the gospel' means—changing our minds about God and lining up behind Jesus, believing that he is God's agent who will re-establish his liberating rule in his world.

2 Kingdom now

Luke 11:14–28

George Ladd, a leading scholar on this theme, summed it up neatly: 'The theology of the kingdom of God is essentially one of conflict and conquest over the kingdom of Satan' (*Theology of the New Testament*, p. 48). Both those elements are evident in today's reading, as they are throughout Jesus' life.

Luke tells the story succinctly: 'Jesus was driving out a demon that was mute' and, of course, confronted by the greater authority of God's Son, 'the demon left' (v. 14). Driving out demons was a regular part of Jesus' ministry, with the Synoptic Gospels reporting four detailed incidents (see Mark 1:21–28; 5:1–20; 7:25–30; 9:14–29) plus many shorter accounts. If God's kingdom was to be re-established, then Satan's stranglehold on people's lives had to be broken and they had to be released from his grip. Exorcisms were the most dramatic showdowns in the clash of powers but they were not the only sort. The healing of diseases (which were not always blamed on demons) was just as important. In each case, Jesus triumphs in the conflict, proving himself able to expel the 'strong man' who has illegitimately occupied God's household (vv. 21–22).

Jesus wisely points out, however, that having expelled the intruder it is foolish to leave the house empty (vv. 24–26): the rightful king needs to take possession through his spirit. As we know from recent military conflicts, getting rid of tyrants is one thing, but reconstructing the peace is another. There's plenty to follow, under God's rule, in the rebuilding of the lives that Satan has tyrannised.

All this was evidence that the kingdom had arrived (v. 20). Astonishingly, though, not everyone welcomed it. The things people saw Jesus doing were not everyday occurrences and so, perhaps, they were puzzled, but some eagerly jumped to the wrong conclusion and attributed his work to Satan. Jesus easily pointed out how foolish such a verdict was (vv. 17–19) and led them to see that God was at work in the things he was doing. Even so, the conflict, both with demons and humans, was to follow Jesus throughout his ministry and lead him, inevitably in the end, to the cross.

3 Upside-down kingdom

Matthew 18:1–5; 20:16, 20–28

The kingdom of God was quite unlike any other kingdom that people had ever encountered. It turned customary ways of working, thinking and measuring value on their heads. People struggled to understand it, and still do: it is profoundly countercultural.

Today's readings illustrate this from three different angles. First, Jesus sets out how to become a citizen in his kingdom. If seeking citizenship in this world, you'd try to prove what an asset you would be, what skills you'd bring, how moral you were, what you'd achieved and how privileged the kingdom would be to have you as a subject. In God's kingdom, these are liabilities rather than assets. The only way in is by becoming 'like little children' (18:3). Preachers have waxed lyrical on the innocence and trusting nature of children (clearly, never having had children of their own!) but Jesus' point is different. He didn't live in a child-centred age. Back then, children were nonentities, not worthy of much attention, still less regarded as having anything to offer. They were generally thought to be empty-handed members of society.

Second, Jesus announces the central principle of his kingdom: 'the last will be first, and the first will be last' (20:16). Those who believe themselves to be at the head of the queue because they're righteous or religious people with whom God is bound to be pleased will find themselves at the rear. Ahead of them, God, in his grace, receives those who don't qualify according to the moral and religious standards of the day. Sinners, failures and the religiously despised receive the priority welcome in his kingdom.

Third, Jesus applies the same upside-down thinking to leadership.

People thought of leaders as being strong, ruling by might, throwing their weight around and vaunting their status, but greatness in God's kingdom is measured by how lowly a servant one is (20:20–28). The advantage, as Martin Luther King said, is that 'by giving this definition of greatness, it means that everybody can be great, because everybody can serve'.

No wonder the disciples found it hard to get their heads around this idea, as well as myriad other features of his kingdom, such as forgiving offenders, loving enemies and going the second mile. But there's no way to be a citizen of this kingdom except to be subject to the laws of this king.

4 Kingdom emissaries

Luke 9:1–6; 10:1–12

No king rules in splendid isolation: all monarchs have servants, messengers and ambassadors. Some people say to God, 'I'd like to serve you, but only in an advisory capacity', but he has no need of advisers in his court. In creating and ruling the world, he is altogether wise and self-sufficient (Isaiah 40:14), but he does appoint emissaries to carry on his mission and extend his kingdom.

The original emissaries were the Twelve, whom Jesus commissioned 'to proclaim the kingdom of God' (9:2). He sent them out with his 'authority' (v. 1): they were not sent into enemy territory to carry on the battle against Satan without the necessary resources. They would have been useless fighting in their own wisdom or strength.

Jesus explains the nature of his commission. It involves using words and working wonders (9:1–2). In any war, words are important—hence the battle for the airwaves and the use of propaganda. Words are important in the battle for God's kingdom, too, not as propaganda but so that people might understand what they are witnessing and grasp their need to come under God's rule. The words are to be accompanied by exorcisms and healings: words are necessary but insufficient on their own. Miracles still have their place today, but so do other forms of wonderful works.

Jesus also gives the Twelve instructions as to how to handle themselves. They are not to rely on their usual means of support, taking everything they need with them; instead, they must trust completely in him. They are to focus on the people who welcome them and not waste time on those who are so under the control of Satan that they reject God's messengers. Battles involve being strategic and not wasting precious resources, and the battle for God's kingdom is no different.

This ambassadorial commission was not confined to the Twelve. The next chapter tells us that Jesus despatched 'seventy-two others' (10:1) with similar orders. Their presence will mean that 'the kingdom of God has come near' those they encounter (vv. 9, 11). Anyone who rejects these messengers will be denying the legitimate king his right to reign over them and so will be inviting his judgement against them (v. 12).

God still goes on sending out his kingdom emissaries.

5 Kingdom come

Matthew 6:9–13

However much the kingdom of God was present in Jesus, it was plain that it had not fully come. God was not yet ruling universally; nor was his rule unchallenged. The Gospels suggest that there is a future aspect to God's kingdom: it is yet to come in its fullness.

To see this, we need look no further than 'the Lord's Prayer'. There, Jesus teaches his disciples to pray, 'Your kingdom come', so obviously it has not yet arrived in its totality. The Jewish people believed in two ages— the present age, characterised by evil, and the age to come, in which God's ideal would be realised. In Jesus that new age had already begun (there was plenty of evidence to demonstrate that) but there was still more to come. His disciples then, as now, lived in the overlap between these two ages, in the tension between the 'already' and 'not yet'.

This is not really difficult to understand. Shortly after Germany was reunited, I stayed in a part of the country that had been East Germany. The telephone system hadn't caught up with the reality, though: ringing a friend in the old West Germany, I still had to make an international telephone call. I was living in the overlap.

So Jesus teaches his disciples to pray that God's kingdom will fully arrive, explained in the next line as the time when God's will is done 'on earth as it is in heaven'. No one can pray that prayer without becoming conscious of the part they play in hastening the arrival of that ultimate kingdom. Living in the overlap, we're called to live now, as much as we can, as we shall live then. If God's perfect kingdom is to be a kingdom of righteousness, justice, grace, peace and purity, then we should get in training and display those qualities in our personal, work, social and political lives too.

Picturing that future kingdom as a time when the whole universe sings in praise of God who reigns supreme, Tom Wright once wrote, 'We are called to learn [this song] and practise it now so as to be ready when the conductor brings down his baton.' Praying 'your kingdom come' is a commitment to join in the choir practice.

6   Kingdom consummation

Matthew 25:31–46

Various sayings of Jesus look forward to the coming of the kingdom of God. Some (such as Matthew 16:28; 24:34; 26:29) are puzzling, implying that the king will enter his kingdom in the very near future, with some of those present witnessing it. People have taken these verses as references to Jesus' death, resurrection or ascension, or to Pentecost or Jerusalem's destruction in AD70, and perhaps the sayings were designed for a fluid interpretation.

Whatever those sayings mean, it is also clear, as in today's reading, that the disciples looked beyond more immediate events to the great climax of history, 'when the Son of Man comes in his glory' (v. 31), is enthroned before all the nations and exercises final judgement. These sayings about his future rule reach back to Daniel 7:13–14, where 'one like a son of man' was given 'authority, glory and sovereign power' over all nations, where his enthronement heralded 'an everlasting dominion' and ushered in an indestructible kingdom.

This kingdom necessarily involves banishing all evil and a final judgement on all wickedness. In Matthew, Jesus speaks of it in terms of separating the 'sheep' from the 'goats' on the basis of how they have treated him. People's reaction to him is betrayed in the way they treat his 'brothers and sisters' (v. 40), by which he probably means his disciples, rather than just anybody, although not all would agree.

Other New Testament writers share this vision of the king's final universal triumph but they express it in different ways. For Paul, it is 'the day of Christ Jesus' (Philippians 1:6; 2:16), an idea rooted in the Old Testament's 'day of the Lord'. It is about conquering all opposition (1 Corinthians 15:20–28; 2 Thessalonians 2:5–12) and bringing everything under God's control. For Peter, it is about 'the day of the Lord' and the renewal of heaven and earth (2 Peter 3). For John, it's about everlasting judgement being meted out on Satan and the banishment of wickedness as God takes his place in the new creation among his people (Revelation 20:7—22:21). However they express it, all these writers speak of judgement on wickedness, the salvation of God's people and God's final, irreversible triumph.

In the light of this, perhaps we should pray more regularly, 'Marana tha', 'Come, Lord Jesus'.

Guidelines

- Give thanks for the signs of God's kingdom at work that you see.
- Have you enlisted in the revolutionary army? Are you living as a subject of King Jesus?
- Think about the ways in which 'the strong man' holds people captive today. What practical steps can you take to assist in their release?
- Consider the place of miracles today and what other wonders may witness to God's power in the world.
- Pray to God concerning those who, as kingdom emissaries, are in the thick of the battle today.
- Pray slowly over the Lord's Prayer, contemplating the implication of each phrase for your own life.
- Use the ancient Christian prayer Marana tha, 'Come, Lord'. What does the prayer mean to you? Are you eager to welcome the returning king?

1 The sower and the seed

Matthew 13:1–23

Preachers are often told that Jesus taught in parables because stories are easy to understand, so they should adopt the same approach—but that's not quite true. The strange thing about the parables is that the disciples often did not understand them and had to ask for an interpretation. Jesus himself said that he used them precisely because they were not accessible to all, so that the secrecy of the kingdom would be guarded (vv. 10–13). This secrecy was about the subversive nature of God's kingdom and the need for Jesus to ensure that his hearers did not pressurise him into being the wrong sort of king.

The leading parable in Matthew's series about the kingdom is of a sower who, like any farmer of his time, broadcasts seed widely. Some of the seed will never yield a crop because it lands on a hard path or on rocky soil or among dense weeds. Such seed gets eaten by birds, scorched by the sun or strangled by the weeds. But the point of the parable is that whatever the hindrances and obstacles, some seed falls on fertile soil and, to varying degrees, produces a handsome crop.

Jesus' kingdom appeared to be powerfully advancing, but it would meet plenty of setbacks and disappointments. Not all who heard about it would respond positively. Satan prevented some from doing so, while some were involved just briefly, and still others were so full of themselves—either their problems or achievements—that they never benefited from it. Yet—and this is the real point—whatever the setbacks, it will produce a harvest, so we must keep on sowing.

Recently some mission thinkers have encouraged a more strategic targeting of the gospel message, so as to increase the effectiveness of the church, but perhaps this parable suggests that the God of the kingdom is profligate in making the good news known widely. Others have spoken as if we can expect everyone to become disciples if only we market the message relevantly, but, again, this parable suggests otherwise. Jesus is much more realistic than some well-meaning inspirational speakers today. The message will always prove divisive, but, in spite of that, it will always produce a harvest among those who perceive its truth.

2 The weeds

Matthew 13:24–30, 36–43

Living in an agricultural economy, it was natural for Jesus to tell stories about farmers and fields. The second story in Matthew's collection of kingdom parables concerns a farmer who sowed good seed but 'while everyone was sleeping, his enemy came and sowed weeds among the wheat' (v. 25). This idea may seem obvious and familiar to us but it baffled his disciples, who asked for an explanation (v. 36) and received it (vv. 37–42).

Several things are notable. The sower is called the Son of Man (vv. 37, 41), which was Jesus' favourite title for himself. It avoided the political traps that other titles involved, and, for those with 'ears to hear', placed him at the scene portrayed in Daniel 7:9–14, where 'one like a son of man' is given dominion. Then, although this parable is usually taken to suggest that we should all put up with a mixed church, composed of saints *and* sinners, it isn't about the church but about the kingdom. It has implications for the church but Jesus is speaking of the dynamic of the kingdom, which is larger than the church. His kingdom doesn't spread through safe, pure communities but out there in the midst of a messy world. Furthermore, pick up the signal he gives: the seed grew 'while everyone was sleeping' (v. 25). God is at work unaided and often unseen. We have our part to play in sowing the seed, but God builds his kingdom in ways that are beyond us. It doesn't all depend on us, as we often arrogantly think (see 1 Corinthians 3:6–8). We only have to think about the gospel's progress in lands that are closed to missionaries to see this truth.

The essential message of the parable is that kingdom advance will always meet with hostility. There is an enemy prowling around, seeking to ruin the work of God, both directly and through his followers (vv. 38–39). We should not underestimate him or expect to escape his hostility. However, the enemy will be dealt with in the end. Many of Jesus' followers wanted his first act to be one of judgement, but this parable teaches us neither to rush to premature judgement nor to take the law into our own hands. The Son of Man and his angels will sort things out at the ultimate judgement (vv. 40–43).

3 The mustard seed and yeast

Matthew 13:31–35

It really is incredible, isn't it? It seems highly improbable that God would rescue the world and make it right again, expelling alien, destructive powers from it and re-establishing his righteous rule, through a wandering rabbi from Nazareth and his bunch of nobody disciples—and especially that he would do it through the execution of that rabbi by a powerful alliance of evil authorities, both seen and unseen. But that was God's plan, and that is what happened in Jesus Christ.

It was the totally improbable nature of the success of God's kingdom that led Jesus to tell the two parables in today's reading. You only have to look to the natural world, Jesus says, to realise that amazing surprises occur in it, so why should the kingdom of God be any different? The mustard seed (vv. 31–32) is a proverbially tiny seed and yet can grow into a huge plant (even if the word 'tree' is a parabolic exaggeration). It might seem ludicrous, but it happens. Similarly, yeast mixed into dough (v. 33) is hidden and unremarkable and yet it catalyses the growth of a large loaf.

In the same way, God's kingdom may seem insignificant in the 'real' world of power-brokers; it may be hidden from people in the world of politics and economics, scientific research and technological development, peace conferences and 'save the planet' colloquies. People may think that the answers all lie in human hands. How could the kingdom that Jesus established achieve anything, especially in view of the way it began and the people he used to start it? Yet surprises happen, and within decades Christ's followers were turning the world upside down, so that today, in every corner of our globe, there are citizens of Christ's kingdom who are having an impact on the world for good.

We should not be surprised when this kingdom, which began in such an insignificant way and whose progress still remains largely hidden to people, reaches its culmination and God rules sovereignly and visibly over all.

4 The hidden treasure and the pearl

Matthew 13:44–46

When Brenda Caunter lost her wedding ring in an allotment in 1972, she and her husband searched frantically for it for some days without success. They never forgot it but they never expected to find it again, either. Forty-one years later, a neighbour was searching the field with a metal detector and discovered it. Brenda's reaction was one of unbelief, mixed with overwhelming delight.

Fortunately Brenda's neighbour was more honest than the man Jesus spoke of, who found hidden treasure in a field. He kept his discovery secret until he could realise all his assets to buy the field and own the treasure for himself. Of course, in telling this parable, Jesus isn't commenting on the man's morality. He's telling a story that people can relate to, to make a simple point: when you find something extremely valuable that's within your grasp, you will do anything to own it. You don't hang on to things of lesser worth when the greatest prize demands all. You trade in your smaller investments and organise your whole life around the big one, making it the priority that puts everything else in the shade.

The same point is made by Jesus' second illustration (hardly a 'parable' at all, really). Any trader in precious stones will sink all their assets into buying one stone if it is priceless. Who will be content with keeping cheap stones if one great prize is available? We may speculate as to whether the jeweller bought it to enjoy for himself or as an investment, but such speculation misses the point. We're prepared to pay great costs to gain great rewards.

The point is obvious, isn't it? If we really understand the extraordinary value of the kingdom that, in Christ, has invaded our world and is in the process of recapturing that world for God—extraordinary value not just for ourselves or even for other people, but for creation itself—we will be prepared to sacrifice anything to make its business our priority. Our involvement in this kingdom can never be a leisure-time pursuit, reserved for occasional attention when we've nothing better to do. It should be all-consuming. What is the point of gaining this whole transient world, rather than devoting all our energies to the one kingdom that will endure for ever?

5 The net

After farming, fishing was the most important industry in Israel in Jesus' time. Several of his inner circle were fishermen and, when he called them, he called them to 'to fish for people' rather than the edible fish of Galilee (Matthew 4:19). The Gospels tell of their continuing fishing activity and of Jesus preaching from their boats, so it's quite natural that, having talked about farmers and fields, he would tell a story about fishing.

It is too much to claim that every parable only makes one point, as was once believed, but some of them, like today's, are just as simple as that. When fishermen come ashore, they sort out their catch, selling the good fish and disposing of the useless ones. So, Jesus says, 'it will be at the end of the age' when the angels will do the separating, disposing of the wicked in 'the blazing furnace, where there will be weeping and gnashing of teeth' (vv. 49–50).

This simple story takes the parable of the weeds one stage further, with numerous and profound implications. The kingdom is about fishing for people—that is, capturing them for God's service. Does the church, as the agent of the kingdom, always recognise this as its calling? Rather than being like a fishing boat, the church sometimes looks more like a battleship with the guns trained on herself; a cruise ship, affording comfortable leisure opportunities; or a galleon, living in the past.

The essential truth of the parable is that it's not our duty to sort people out here and now, deciding who's in and who's out. God's agents will do so when the kingdom reaches its fulfilment. There is a final judgement to come, when true justice will be delivered, and we are wise to leave that safely to God. Why are we so prone to engage in 'Operation throw them out' here on earth?

The parable, although metaphorical, also contains the most terrible and real warning for those who have not actively lived as God's subjects. The final fate of 'the wicked' is a dreadful one, to be avoided at all costs. Jesus never promises anywhere that 'all will be saved in the end' but rather that everlasting separation from God, sometimes called hell, is an awful reality.

6 The wedding banquet

Matthew 22:1–14

This parable is the final one in a trio that Matthew has put together (Matthew 21:28—22:14) and integrates the themes of the previous two. It bristles with insights rather than making a single point, especially as Matthew's telling of it adds to Luke's version (Luke 14:16–24). Think about its teaching.

First, the kingdom of God is a banquet. Since the Passover, Israel had marked special celebrations with food. Isaiah prophesied a future banquet of the Messiah (Isaiah 25:6) when death and suffering would be abolished. The kingdom is not something to be feared, but is a party to enjoy. Secondly, the party is 'ready' (v. 4). As Jesus teaches elsewhere, this stresses that Isaiah's future vision has already begun. We don't have to wait any longer. The kingdom has future implications but it has already started, so get on board!

Thirdly, the expected guests refuse to come (vv. 2–7). Since the banquet celebrates the king's son, you'd expect the important people to want to be seen with the 'in crowd'. Yet some are indifferent and ignore the invitation while others are actually hostile, ill-treating the king's messengers. The story is a thinly disguised pointer to the religious establishment who rejected Christ.

Fourthly, the guests who do come are a surprising crowd (vv. 8–10). The ordinary folk now invited are nothing special. In fact some of them are downright disreputable. But God's kingdom is composed of such people rather than the self-conscious goody-goodies and religiously respectable. Fifthly, even they can't take the invitation casually (vv. 11–14). They are expected to show respect and come in clean clothes (not posh wedding outfits) rather than dirty working clothes. The man who can't be bothered to get changed demonstrates disrespect for the king and shows a lack of understanding that, although he is welcome, a change is required. This is a metaphor for a change of direction in life—in other words, repentance. Far from enjoying the feast, the man finds himself ejected 'into the darkness'.

George Beasley-Murray summarised it like this: 'The banquet is ready, the guests have arrived, the hall is packed, and the feast is in progress.

The arrival of the king constitutes the climax and joy of the occasion. But for one, at least, it is the hour of judgement; since it entails an exclusion which is final, it is *the last hour*' (*Jesus and the Kingdom of God*, p. 122).

Guidelines

- Use your own experience to reflect on the types of soil on which the seed falls. Have you known disappointments and setbacks? Were there things you could have done differently to prevent them? Are you rejoicing in a harvest and thanking God for it?
- Examine your own attitudes. Are you quick to rush to judgement, especially about others in the church?
- Give thanks for the unexpected and revolutionary changes you have witnessed in your lifetime, such as the downfall of communism and apartheid. Were these signs of the kingdom? What hope do they give for the future?
- Just as we do an annual financial audit, why not do a spiritual audit of your life, asking particularly how much you really value God's kingdom and how much of your life revolves around it?
- Picture your church as a ship. What kind of ship image captures your church best?
- Several of the parables speak of a final judgement. Since we live in a very tolerant culture, how remote or how realistic do you find this idea? How might you explain it to others so as to remove any defensiveness they may feel?

FURTHER READING

G.R. Beasley-Murray, *Jesus and the Kingdom of God*, Paternoster Press, 1986.

R.T. France, *Divine Government*, SPCK, 1990.

George Ladd, *A Theology of the New Testament*, Eerdmans, 1993.

Tom Wright, *How God Became King*, SPCK, 2012.

Ecclesiastes

Who was Ecclesiastes? The name is the Greek version of the Hebrew title Qohelet, and it literally means 'the one who assembles people together', generally translated as 'the Teacher', or 'the Preacher'. The book that bears this name is part of the 'Wisdom tradition' in the Old Testament, and is ascribed to wise King Solomon, 'the son of David, king in Jerusalem' (Ecclesiastes 1:1). However, the language and content of Ecclesiastes suggest that it originates from a much later teacher than Solomon, someone who was critical of many of the conclusions of the Wisdom tradition that had gone before. For example, although Ecclesiastes mentions God quite frequently, he's presented not as creator of a good and meaningful world where virtue is rewarded, but as a shadowy presence, indifferent or cruel towards the human lot. This is very unlike the picture we have of Solomon receiving wisdom from God as a gift of covenantal love (see 1 Kings 3:11–14).

So, who was Qohelet, 'the Teacher'? Was he a real teacher whose work was published by a disciple with a few editorial comments, or was he, like Kahlil Gibran's 'Prophet', a fictional teacher, into whose mouth an author put his own thoughts?

Scholars answer this question in different ways. I shall treat Ecclesiastes as the teaching of one man, Qohelet, with a small element of comment from another, because that's how the book presents itself. But there are other difficult questions, too, to consider, such as what does the repeated phrase 'Vanity of vanities' mean and (hardest of all) why is a book with such a negative image of God included in the Bible?

Although rabbis were still questioning its inspiration in AD90, it was nevertheless generally treated as an authoritative part of Jewish religious heritage by that time, and would have been well known to Jesus. It was accepted as scripture by the early Christians, and comes to us as something we must wrestle with.

Unless otherwise stated, quotations are taken from the New Revised Standard Version of the Bible.

1 A melancholy life

Ecclesiastes 1

This chapter gives an overview of human life in poetic language, but with utterly negative conclusions. Qohelet's signature phrase, 'Vanity of vanities', sets the tone for all that follows. Scholars render the word translated in the NRSV as 'vanity' with a variety of other abstract terms: futility, absurdity, meaninglessness and enigma. The underlying Hebrew word is *hevel*, which probably originally meant 'an exhalation of breath', as distinct from the life-force of breath that we draw into ourselves (*ruach*). *Hevel*, then, expresses the emptiness of waste. We should remember this Hebrew root, because its concrete imagery reminds us that Ecclesiastes is not a product of Greek philosophy, although some have found Greek influences in it.

The opening passage suggests that life is a pointless treadmill experienced among cycles of nature that are leading nowhere. Shockingly, it associates the unhappy 'vanity' of human life with God's intention (vv. 13–14); we usually think of God in the light of Genesis 1's repeated assertion that what he made was 'good'. Some might argue that 'God' in Ecclesiastes bears little resemblance to the God made known elsewhere in the Hebrew scriptures, or to the Father of our Lord Jesus Christ. Qohelet's 'God' seems like someone who sets creation going but heartlessly retires from its ongoing life into shadowy distance.

However, a mysteriously dark side to God crops up elsewhere in the scriptures: he is one who condemns Adam and Eve to toil, frustration and dust (Genesis 3:16–19); one who declares 'I form light and create darkness, I make weal and create woe' (Isaiah 45:7). It would take the apostle Paul, echoing the language of Ecclesiastes, to set the thought of a God who has 'subjected the creation to futility' within the context of redemptive hope (Romans 8:20).

2 A man at odds with himself?

Here we see what look like two sides of Qohelet's personality. He has the capacity, apparently, to throw himself into enjoyment and work and find genuine pleasure in them (v. 10b), while also being inclined to step back from experience and weigh up whether it has lasting value—an exercise leading to despair and hatred of life (vv. 18–20). The second side creates the mood overshadowing the whole book, and yet the capacity for enjoyment and for finding in work its own reward breaks through frequently as well. If Ecclesiastes is a chronological record of Qohelet's teaching, we might think that he had a psychological condition swinging between happiness and depression, as many people do.

However, there may be more to it than this: Qohelet may be skilfully using the tool of irony to subvert what he sees as an over-simplistic understanding of wisdom. He identifies himself with Solomon through his claim to have had vast wealth, and yet he subverts the idea that such magnificence is inextricably bound up with a godly kind of wisdom (as it is presented in 1 Kings 3:10–14), by picturing himself as someone who, in his wealth, positively chooses to experiment with self-indulgence (v. 10a) and call that 'wisdom'. In this context, 'wisdom' is not the source of a good life, rooted in God, but an attitude that self-consciously tries everything out and then pronounces everything to be nothing but 'vanity and a chasing after wind' (v. 11).

Perhaps we are being shown the inner conflict of someone who found the traditional concept of wisdom, with its belief in balance in the universe, attractive yet impossible; he may have felt he had to expose it as such through irony, in the face of life's evidence. How much modern irony and hedonism are rooted in similar disillusionment?

3 God or fate?

The first eight poetic verses of chapter 3 make a popular reading for funerals and memorial services, but what do they mean? That God is purposeful and good, and nothing happens outside his timing and plan? Or that wisdom consists in learning to discern the right time for action or for inaction? Or simply that 'things happen', irrespective of us, in the cyclical way described in 1:4–9, and we should just learn to submit to what time brings, whether joy and happiness or labour and loss?

Pete Seeger took these words and turned them into a song in the 1950s, covered by The Byrds in the 1960s. In his song, the refrain 'Turn, turn, turn' suggests a cyclical, almost fated pattern to life, but the final line 'I swear it's not too late', added by Seeger after the phrase 'a time for peace', suggests that there are choices that human beings can and should make to amend life's circumstances.

It may be that Qohelet took a pre-existing poem which taught that wisdom lies in discerning the behaviour appropriate to differing times, and (as in the previous chapter) subjected it to irony by setting it within his own despairing conclusions about the vanity of all we do (v. 9) and the cyclical and repetitive patterns of the world (v. 15).

The sense that everything is out of our hands is reinforced in this chapter by its frequent references to God—not a God who intimately cares about us but one who wishes to overawe us and prove that we are no different from animals in our origins and destiny (v. 19). In other words, this is a God who seems to have much in common with cruel Fate.

Yet Qohelet does leave the door slightly ajar to more hopeful beliefs: many translations of verse 11 speak not of 'a sense of past and future' (NRSV) in our hearts, but a sense of 'eternity', put there by God (NIV). Then, although it does not pronounce a verdict, verse 21 leaves open the possibility that 'the human spirit goes upwards' when it dies. Qohelet finds this difficult to believe, but allows that the possibility might be there.

4 Bright spots in an otherwise futile life

Ecclesiastes 4

When we watch or read the daily news, it's hard to disagree with Qohelet's melancholy and negative view of life. In verse 1 he summarises what he sees—'all the oppressions that are practised under the sun', power in the hand of the oppressors, and no comfort for the oppressed (an observation that is stressed by repetition). It is better never to have lived than to experience such a world, he concludes (vv. 2–3). Even when he turns his mind to work—an activity that he so often holds up as a source of satisfaction—Qohelet now talks about how it is motivated only by envy. The skills that we admire draw their energy from human competitiveness (v. 4). He is no doubt overstating his case in a blanket statement like this, but no one can deny what a large part the desire to outstrip others does play in spurring people on to achievement.

Even if work is based on 'vanity', though, it remains unavoidable. An indolent life leads to self-destruction (v. 5), yet it would be better to be satisfied with a little than to 'chase after wind' as a workaholic (v. 6). There is real wisdom here in Qohelet's observation of our dilemmas about work, but he frames it all in the comfortless thought that a person without heirs is, in the end, working for nothing (v. 7). As they say, 'you can't take it with you when you go'.

This leads him to reflect on where we may find comfort in this futile world, and he finds it in human relationships (vv. 9–12). He also finds something to admire in the poor youth who may turn out to be wiser than 'an old but foolish king, who will no longer take advice' (v. 13). Yet, in admiring the one, he highlights the melancholy decline of the other, and even the admirable youth, should he attain power, cannot please the people for ever (v. 16; compare 1:11).

Once again, it seems that Qohelet's observation of the ways of the world leads to despairing conclusions about their ultimate meaninglessness, even though, along the way of life, we may find genuine comfort in one another.

5 Good advice for bad circumstances

Ecclesiastes 5

Despite his assessment of life as futile, Qohelet still feels it worthwhile to issue practical teaching about human conduct. From now onwards, we begin to find, interspersed with his more general observations on life, proverbs similar to those in other Wisdom literature—adages addressed to the young, to set them on the right way.

Qohelet addresses the issue of proper reverence before God. Verse 1 probably means that obedience is better than sacrifice, as the concept of 'listening' is very close to that of obeying (see 1 Samuel 15:22).

Obedience is frequently commended in the Bible; so too are there frequent warnings against the rash use of words (see vv. 2–7). The issue of making vows rashly ('taking the Lord's name in vain') was very immediate for the ancient Hebrews, because a vow was a recognised way of strengthening supplication—a kind of bargaining chip—and sometimes involved drastic personal consequences (see Judges 11:30–31, 34–35; 1 Samuel 1:11). In linking dreams with cares and empty verbosity, Qohelet may be warning against attempts at divination through dreams. One way or another, attempting to get a handle on one's future, either through making vows or attempting divination, is a waste of time. It is better simply to have a sober fear of God (v. 7).

From rash utterances, Qohelet moves to issues of corruption and money: he sees corrupt government as inevitable, but it is better than no government at all for an agricultural nation needing defence (vv. 8–9). The love of money is portrayed as a false path (v. 10); its possession has ambivalent consequences (v. 11), it is easily lost (vv. 13–15), and its pursuit oppresses the spirit (v. 17).

Once again, then, he recommends the simple enjoyment of life and its pleasures (including work). To be able to live like this is the 'gift of God' (v. 19), if only because it is a distraction from brooding on life's brevity and emptiness (v. 20). This seems a bleak assessment, and yet a heart well occupied can experience 'joy'.

6 Dissatisfaction

Ecclesiastes 6

Chapter 6 is the continuation of Qohelet's reflections at the end of chapter 5. Sadly, however, we find here that what might have looked like a hopeful possibility—the enjoyment of simple pleasures, which there he called 'the gift of God'—is something that God apparently capriciously denies to some people (v. 2). By invoking the image of a stillborn child and calling it happier than the dissatisfied rich man, Qohelet could scarcely be making his point more strongly (vv. 3–6). In a similar way, Job invoked the idea of the stillborn child when his extreme suffering caused him to curse the day he was born (Job 3:11–19).

On a first reading, we might think that the painful dissatisfaction described by Qohelet is caused by outward circumstances—for example, when a rich man loses all he has to 'a stranger' (v. 2). As we read on, however, it becomes clear that this is not what he is saying. The agony of dissatisfaction may smite someone who has many years in which to enjoy his wealth and many heirs to pass it on to (v. 3). Only the reference to having no (proper) burial suggests an outward circumstance—perhaps a breakdown in relationships with children—which might be a source of pain. Yet Qohelet's key thought about dissatisfaction seems to be in verse 7: appetite is not satisfied. Inward contentment seems impossible for some people. Their desire 'wanders', even when they should able to feast their eyes happily on what is in front of them (v. 9), and people who suffer thus may just as easily be among 'the wise' (in Qohelet's terms: see 2:9) as the 'foolish'.

The last few verses of this chapter are rather obscure; they argue the fruitlessness of dispute—but with whom? The NRSV plural translation in verse 10b ('those who are stronger') probably obscures the thought that the 'one who is stronger' (NIV), with whom it is pointless to dispute, is God. If the latter interpretation is correct, we have another instance of fatalist determinism fashioning Qohelet's concept of the ways of God with human beings.

Guidelines

The first half of Ecclesiastes seems to have led us down into a vortex of depressing thoughts. Observation of the world, of history and of individual human lives has led Qohelet to the conclusion not only that life is meaningless and 'vain', but also that it is God who has made it so. There are some bright spots in the darkness—most particularly the comfort of strong human relationships (4:9–12); the possibility of finding joy in simple pleasures, including one's work (2:24–25; 3:12–13; 5:18–20), and the possibility of merit being recognised and overcoming weak and foolish government (4:14–15). Nevertheless, these things are eclipsed by the impermanence and cyclical nature of life. Death comes to all, and nobody's memory lasts for ever. Only God and his doings endure (2:14), and he seems capricious in the ways in which he allots joy and happiness to humankind.

We may feel that the lack of 'good news' means that this book has little to teach us, but it is important to stick with it. Ecclesiastes is perhaps an essential antidote to the relentless cheerfulness of some versions of religion. Its searing honesty may invite us to admit our own doubts and difficulties with faith, given the facts of the world around us, and its presence in the canon may reassure us that there is a place among God's people even for those who are depressed or cynical—maybe for *us*, when we are hitting rock bottom.

Qohelet conducts his experiments with life, his reflections and his teaching, within the presence of God, whom he refers to quite often, but he does not see God through the positive lens of 'salvation history'. This could be because, for a Jew writing some time after the return from exile, the reality of 'salvation' back in the promised land falls so very far short of the visions of the prophets. So God is not a sympathetic figure for Qohelet—but he is there.

As Christians, we hope for a different kind of salvation, but, in hoping, we need to be realistic enough to face up to all the disappointments and disillusionment that life brings. Our vision of God needs also to be big enough to make space for the agonising mysteries and difficulties of creation, without glossing them over.

1 Pessimism or realism?

Ecclesiastes 7

Qohelet reverts to the traditional format of aphorisms addressed by a wise teacher to the young. His first proverb, about the value of reputation, seems unexceptionable, but immediately leads to a consideration of death (the time when one's reputation is sealed). His preference for mourning over feasting, and sorrow over laughter (vv. 3–4), sits ill with his earlier exhortations to 'eat, drink and be merry' (2:24), although in chapter 7 he is portraying drunken mirth in particular, for the word translated as 'feasting' in verse 2 might better be translated as 'carousing'. His gloomy preference for 'the house of mourning' suggests that we should intentionally look death's reality in the face, rather than try to avoid it in pursuing pleasure. Is this a realistic attitude or merely pessimistic? Verse 14 suggests that there must be a middle way—a proper level of enjoyment when life goes well, alongside sober acceptance of adversity.

Verses 7–12 are a series of proverbs, full of good sense, which would sit well in any collection, but with verses 13 and 14 Qohelet's adverse view of God breaks through: God has made things 'crooked' in order to baffle us. The 'crookedness' of things is demonstrated by the fact that people do not get their just deserts (v. 15).

The second half of the chapter shows the fruit of this view of life, as Qohelet mingles aphorisms with reflections in a more personal form. He counsels against idealism as much as against self-destructive wickedness (vv. 16–17). A person who fears the kind of God that Qohelet believes in 'will avoid all extremes' (v. 18, NIV). Just as total righteousness is unattainable (v. 20), so too, it turns out, is total wisdom (vv. 23–25). Then (in a move common among those who justify their own imperfections), he savagely attacks the 'other'—in this case, woman the temptress (v. 26), generalising from one bad experience to all women (v. 28). Balance reasserts itself, however, in verse 29, where he at least partly exonerates both God and women: it is humanity in general that has chosen crookedness over straightforwardness.

There seems to be some confusion here, as though we were seeing an inner conflict in Qohelet between his role as a teacher of traditional wisdom, with its positive message that there is a good way to live, and his personal disillusionment with both morality and the quest for understanding.

2 Wisdom's limitations

Ecclesiastes 8

A sense of Qohelet's confusion persists into this chapter. It opens with what looks like a paean of praise for the traditional wise man who knows how to interpret things. Wisdom can apparently be so internalised that it almost shines out of such a person (v. 1). And yet, by verses 16 and 17, Qohelet's conviction that we have no capacity to understand anything that happens has reappeared. Even the person who applies himself tirelessly to 'know wisdom' makes only an empty claim if he says he can interpret the ways of God and the events of history. So much for the wise man!

Between the statements of these opposing ideas are reflections on prudent behaviour in a hierarchical society, and further observations on the unjust outcomes to people's lives. Perhaps wisdom amounts to not much more than prudence—knowledge of how to 'keep your back covered' through unquestioning obedience in the presence of arbitrary power (vv. 2–5), and acquiescence in the face of the unavoidable, without the illusion that moral equivocation might help us avoid it (vv. 6–8).

As for justice, Qohelet's experience shows that there is little of it about. Hypocrisy is rewarded with long life (v. 10), and delays in due punishment only encourage a fixed habit of wickedness (v. 11). If this latter comment were simply an observation on the failure of human justice systems to expedite conviction and sentencing, it would stand as a useful piece of social comment. However, given Qohelet's earlier conclusions, we must infer that he has divine dilatoriness also in view. He struggles with this: he wants to believe that the balance of conduct and reward will eventually be restored (vv. 12–13), but the measure of ultimate judgement, he says, will be 'fear before God'. Given his earlier reflections, the God whom Qohelet thinks we should fear is probably as arbitrary as the human king who 'does whatever he pleases' (v. 3).

No wonder, then, that he sums up the inequities of life by again using the word 'vanity' (perhaps best translated here as 'an enigma', v. 14), and falls back once more on his somewhat despairing recommendation to take what enjoyment in life is available (v. 15).

3 Death takes all

Qohelet was not an atheist, but he was certainly one who denied a doctrine that was becoming established in Israel after the exile—belief in life after death. Given this denial, the hope he expressed in the previous chapter, that those who fear God will eventually be rewarded and those who do not will meet their condemnation, looks extremely feeble.

Today's chapter begins with a statement that he 'laid to heart' everything that experience and reflection had shown him (as expressed in the previous chapters), and the result was that he came to a point where he could be confident of nothing—not even of God's preferential love for the 'righteous and the wise' (v. 1). Since they experience the same fate as the wicked and irreligious, there is really nothing to be preferred in human life to the simple fact of being alive and self-conscious rather than dead and unconscious (vv. 4–6).

Bleak though this conclusion is, it at least expresses a more positive outlook than the one voiced earlier in the book, preferring the fate of the stillborn child to that of the person burdened with dissatisfaction (6:3–5). By facing up to the brute fact of death, which comes to all without warning, whatever their attributes (vv. 11–12), a certain equanimity can be gained, within which a limited, practical wisdom is possible, not to mention a relatively happy life—even in the company of a woman (v. 9, *pace* 7:28)!

From this point in the book, we find a series of sayings about this limited, practical wisdom; some of them, standing by themselves, have been found helpful and memorable by subsequent generations—for example, 'Whatever your hand finds to do, do with [all] your might' (v. 10a) is still heard today. 'Wisdom is better than weapons of war' (v. 18) was used as a slogan by women suffragists in the early 20th century and recommends a set of preferences that the nations would do well to follow, even though Qohelet sets these words within a context where there are barbs. The wise peacemaker may die completely unremembered and unappreciated (v. 16), and the peace that he or she creates is extremely vulnerable to the bungling or sin of others (v. 18). All too often, those who make a lot of noise effectively harness the folly of the crowd to a disastrous course (v. 17).

4 Wisdom for living in the social order

Towards the end of Ecclesiastes we are told that Qohelet weighed and studied and arranged many proverbs (12:9): presumably we are now reading part of his collection. There is less in this chapter of his personal philosophising, although his characteristic voice breaks through in verse 14b, warning us of our severely limited knowledge. We are also made sharply aware of his social conservatism in verses 5–7 and 16–17. In his view, 'wisdom' is the natural preserve of the rich and noble, and the reversal of the established social order spells disaster. This tells us that, even if he was not King Solomon, Qohelet belonged to the upper echelons of society in his own day, and the educational system that 'wisdom teachers' represented was probably primarily directed towards the sons of the well-to-do. Within a conservative hierarchical order, Qohelet warns of the dangers of imprudently challenging those more powerful than oneself in even the most covert ways (v. 20).

Given his background, we may be surprised to find proverbs in this list that look like health and safety advice for manual labourers and popular entertainers (vv. 8–11), but some of these sayings are of such obvious banality that perhaps they are really intended to be metaphors for the errors that people make in social conduct.

As is typical in other biblical collections of proverbs, the dominant contrast is between 'wisdom' and 'folly'. We have seen earlier in the book how Qohelet had come to see wisdom in very limited terms, as essentially practical and unable to attain any wide overview of life's purpose or meaning. Folly is set up here as an almost comical characteristic, belonging to those who do not know how to behave appropriately (vv. 2–3, 15); in particular, folly reveals itself in unbridled talkativeness (vv. 12–14). However, Qohelet gives this observation extra depth by implying that loquacity is stupid because of the limitations to our knowledge, which make too much talk inevitably inane (v. 14).

Although he asserts that 'feasts are made for laughter; wine gladdens life' (v. 19), we get the impression that, for all his experiments with hedonism, Qohelet has come to be ill at ease in the easy ebb and flow of conversation after a good dinner!

5 Get on with life

Perhaps the key verse in this chapter is verse 4: 'Whoever observes the wind will not sow; and whoever regards the clouds will not reap.' Qohelet's fatalistic teaching has cast a long shadow over life, with his deep conviction that, in the end, it is meaningless—worth no more than a puff of breath. If his pupils pay too much attention to this gloom, though, nothing will be achieved, even within the narrow confines allowed to human initiative. They just have to 'get on with it'.

'Cast thy bread upon the waters' (v. 1, KJV) was, for a long time, a well-known proverb in our culture, even though its meaning is not entirely clear. Some people see in it a merchant's recommendation to invest widely, and overseas, if you want to make a good return. This would chime in well with the advice to 'divide your means seven ways, or even eight, for you do not know what disaster may happen on earth' (v. 2)—again, prudent advice on maximising gain and minimising risk. Other people, though, understand 'Send out your bread upon the waters' as words about generosity in giving: charity bestowed on others may one day be repaid when you need it. Either way, both these proverbs, together with the one in verse 6, exhorting diligence in work, advise people to live prudent lives of enlightened self-interest, even though nature carries on blindly without regard to us (v. 3) and we do not understand the work and ways of God (v. 5).

The second part of the chapter reverts to Qohelet's theme that we should rejoice, so far as we can, in life and its simple pleasures: even seeing the sun should be enough to lift our hearts (v. 7). Yet he never lets us forget that death and darkness are coming, reducing everything on earth to 'vanity' (v. 8). There seems almost to be a relish in the way in which, in verses 9 and 10, he produces a sting in the tail each time he exhorts young men to enjoy their lives. Once again, the theme of God's judgement appears, even though there is no proof or prognostication given as to when or how this judgement will happen.

We may finish this chapter feeling that we have read some good practical advice, but that it comes from someone who is also projecting outwards some deep inner conflict or confusion.

6 Old age and death

Qohelet's teaching ends in a burst of poetry. Verses 1–7 are reminiscent, in their piled-up metaphors, of other oriental literature, such as *The Rubaiyat of Omar Khayyam* (a collection of verses with a strong emphasis on the brevity of life). Even in translation, the use of the imagery creates its own rhythm in the words, and the ingenuity and elusiveness of the metaphors employed to describe an ageing body and the falling-apart of life's treasures create a sense of mysterious beauty. This is why these verses form a 'purple passage' much beloved of many Bible readers, even though their subject is our sad decline into decrepitude and death.

Sad though the subject is, however, there is a sense of hope here: the very injunction to 'Remember your creator in the days of your youth' at the beginning of the poem (v. 1), coupled with the description of death as the returning of breath 'to God who gave it' (v. 7), begins to hint at the thought that there may be a proper shape to life after all—that we have a destiny in God to live towards. Yet, as if to slap this emerging thought down, Qohelet immediately falls back on his opening and ubiquitous motto: 'Vanity of vanities… all is vanity' (v. 8).

The closing verses of the book (vv. 9–14) are very likely to be an epilogue composed by an editor, both praising Qohelet as a teacher of wisdom and putting his own stamp on the book's meaning. He does this by repeating and emphasising Qohelet's occasional injunctions to 'Fear God' (v. 13), and linking them to his ambiguous and self-contradictory thoughts about God's judgement (v. 14). The editor, no doubt, has the aim of 'tidying up' Qohelet's teaching into a more orthodox moral and theological framework in which God is truly interested in human life, rewarding the good and punishing the evil in a way that is comprehensible as part of the general Wisdom tradition.

Jesus was steeped in all the Wisdom books, and their echoes may be found in his teaching; indeed, the final words of this epilogue may lie behind Jesus' words in Luke 8:17. But our reading of Ecclesiastes may leave us wondering what Jesus made of the bulk and thrust of Qohelet's teaching—and what should we, Christ's followers, make of it?

Guidelines

- Qohelet comes to his conclusions about life's random meaninglessness by the observation of nature and human affairs, yet he clings to the bare notion of God. Many of our contemporaries believe in a random universe, having abandoned the notion of God altogether. They may often seem more cheerful and accepting of things as they are than Qohelet does, yet some of them are sensitive to 'existential despair'. Does the book of Ecclesiastes give us a bridge into understanding and empathising with the despair that lies at the edges of our culture?

- Ecclesiastes, like the book of Job, presents a critique of an oversimplistic view of God and of the consequences of good and evil in human life. At the end of Job, God appears and confounds Job with demonstrations that humankind cannot possibly understand God's ways. How easy is it to live our life of faith with acceptance of God's incomprehensibility and of the many difficult things about the universe that we cannot neatly explain away?

- What difference does our belief in Jesus make when God seems indifferent or far away?

- Is the 'good news' in Ecclesiastes more to be found in some of Qohelet's wise and memorable sayings or in the fact that someone of his temperament and outlook has found a place in the biblical record? Do you know anyone who is like him in any way, and do they have a place in the community of God's people?

FURTHER READING

Robert Alter, *The Wisdom Books, Job, Proverbs and Ecclesiastes: A translation with commentary*, W.W. Norton, 2010.

Craig G. Bartholomew, *Ecclesiastes*, Baker Academic, 2009. (This scholarly work presents a more positive interpretation of Qohelet's beliefs than mine.)

Cross and resurrection in John's Gospel

John's story of Jesus is like a symphony, building up to a remarkable and surprising finale. We begin with snatches of familiar tunes echoing from the past—tunes resounding from the majestic story of God's relationship with his covenant people in the Old Testament. These combine with the somewhat discordant melodies from the future, foretelling Jesus' impending death and resurrection. So the symphony has themes echoing in both directions, themes from the past being picked up and becoming part of the harmony and themes from the future building into a crescendo towards the dramatic finale.

Over the next two weeks, we will listen to a few of those themes as we consider the cross and resurrection in John's account. The Old Testament images combine with those that look forward to the cross and resurrection, to give new meaning to the present narrative of Jesus' own life. To change the metaphor, ripples spread out from both ends of the pond, and where they meet we see something more of who Jesus is. As the ripples of the Old Testament story interact with the ripples of Jesus' impending death and resurrection, we see Jesus' earthly ministry in a new and deeper way.

In the first week, we consider passages from the first half of the Gospel of John. Our first two studies come from chapter 1, where we find indications that the story of Jesus cannot be understood without reference both to the Old Testament and to the cross. In the second week, as we move towards the last hours of Jesus' life, the Old Testament themes continue but there is a shift in emphasis. The cross now explicitly becomes the key to understanding the events that we read. Like a detective novel, the story can be fully understood only in the light of its ending. So in John, as in the other Gospels, narrative time slows down as we focus on the time Jesus spent with his disciples and then observe Jesus' arrest and trial.

Unless otherwise stated, quotations are taken from the New Revised Standard Version of the Bible.

1 We have seen his glory

John 1:10–18

John's account of Jesus' life begins like no other. The majestic prologue takes us back to the beginning. Like the prologue to a Greek drama, the first 18 verses tell us all we need to know to understand the story. If I were telling the story, I would have talked about the glory that the Word had in heaven (and indeed, later on, Jesus does refer to the glory that he had with his Father 'before the world existed': see 17:5), but here John reserves the word 'glory' for the incarnation. With deliberate echoes of the tabernacle in the wilderness (v. 14; Exodus 40:34), John tells us that the Word became flesh and dwelt (or 'pitched his tabernacle') among us.

This remarkable image tells us that, in Jesus, the very presence of God has come to dwell among his people, just as God dwelt with the Israelites on their journey from slavery in Egypt. This is amazing enough, in a world that finds it so easy to keep the divine and the material separate, where God and flesh do not meet, but there is an echo of a more amazing message yet. The glory of God is seen in 'the only begotten'. The echo of Isaac as the only begotten son of Abraham (see Genesis 22:2; Hebrews 11:17, KJV) not only suggests that Isaac is a prototype of the incarnation. It also gives us a hint of the sacrificial death of Jesus, the only begotten, and John tells us that it is in Jesus' role as 'the only begotten' that we have seen his glory.

God's glory is seen in something other than heavenly splendour. It is seen in the Word made flesh. As we read through John's Gospel, we will see that glory is displayed not in power or military might but in God's identification with humanity in the person of his Son, Jesus. Ultimately it is seen in Jesus' self-offering on the cross. On the cross we behold his glory, the glory of the only begotten Son. On the cross Jesus reveals the very character of the Father to us, a character of loving-kindness and faithfulness, grace and truth (vv. 14, 17; see, for example, Psalm 86:15). On the cross we receive from his fullness grace upon grace.

2 Behold, the Lamb of God (1)

John 1:29–42

Certain phrases can conjure up far more than the words themselves, because of their associations. 'We will fight them on the beaches' brings to mind Winston Churchill. 'I have a dream' awakens images of Martin Luther King Jr's vision of a society where people are not divided by race. Likewise, John the Baptist's simple phrase 'the Lamb of God who takes away the sin of the world' (vv. 29, 36) conjures up a whole worldview that helps us understand who Jesus is.

John does not often refer to 'sin' or try to define it, yet, as he begins his story, he gives us an image of a world in which lambs were a regular part of the sacrificial system. Animals, including lambs, were offered to God for all sorts of reasons, mostly associated with failure to keep aspects of the covenant law (for example, Exodus 29:38–39; Leviticus 3—4). This idea may be unfamiliar or even uncomfortable to us but it made perfect sense to those who lived in a culture where transgression of covenantal commitments was a serious business. There needed to be something to take away (to 'expiate') their sins. Animals without blemish or spot were offered for this purpose (see Leviticus 3:1). On the Day of Atonement, the scapegoat wandered off into the desert 'carrying away' the sins of the people with it (Leviticus 16:20–22), and then there was the Passover lamb, signifying God's covenantal protection of his people when he came to judge the Egyptians (Exodus 12).

It is likely that John's words here draw together all such imagery in one simple statement. Jesus is not only the Word made flesh, the only begotten. He is also the Lamb of God who takes away the sin of the world, a world that is remarkable not primarily for its diversity and size but for its hostility and rejection of the one who has come to bring it light (1:10–11). It is this 'Lamb of God' who gives to those who believe in him the power to become children of God (v. 12). It is this 'Lamb of God' who calls us, along with the disciples of John the Baptist, to come and see where he is staying and to remain with him (vv. 39–42).

3 The serpent in the wilderness

John 3:1–21

As students and even teachers of the Bible, we can miss the point. Nicodemus enters our story secretly, acknowledging something special about Jesus and his ministry that can only come from God (v. 2). In an often-debated verse, Jesus tells him that to see the kingdom of God, he must be born again, regenerated from above (v. 3). There follows a discussion, typical of John's writing, where Jesus' questioner takes his words at face value (v. 4) and Jesus then explains them from a heavenly point of view (vv. 5–8). Still confused, Nicodemus asks, 'How can these things be?' (v. 9).

Again, the Old Testament resonates through our reading. Jesus speaks of himself as the Son of Man (v. 13), a term used by the prophet Daniel to refer to the one who would come to establish God's kingdom (Daniel 7:13–14). This Son of Man is then linked with a second Old Testament passage, the strange story of the serpent in the wilderness (Numbers 21:4–9). This story speaks both of God's judgement in sending a plague of snakes among his people because of their impatient grumbling and of his mercy in providing a bronze serpent to heal them. Moses set the serpent on a pole and anyone who was bitten by a snake could look at the bronze serpent and live.

Jesus tells us that, like the serpent, the Son of Man is to be 'lifted up' (v. 14). This phrase most obviously suggests his exaltation, but here it clearly also refers to the literal 'lifting up' of Jesus on the cross. The all-conquering Son of Man will be exalted like the serpent on a pole, and anyone who looks on him will live. Ironically, though, this 'exaltation' will occur in the context of his shameful death on the cross. Echoes of the story of God's covenant in the past combine with hints of Jesus' crucifixion in the future to explain how someone can be born again. The new birth is a life from above that is received as people look to the Son of Man exalted on the cross. Just as those in the wilderness looked at the snake on the pole and lived, so now, whoever looks to the Son of Man will not only live but have eternal life (v. 15).

4 The living bread

Jesus' sermon at Capernaum can only be understood in the light of his impending death. Towards the end of the sermon, in answer to questions from the Jewish leaders, Jesus speaks of those who feed on his flesh and drink his blood (v. 56). Whether these words should be seen as 'sacramental' or not is debated. Whichever view we take, it is clear that the words tell us something about the disciples' need to identify with Jesus' impending death and so to find nourishment.

As we have seen in previous examples, the image doesn't only look forward; it also looks back. The sermon and debate take place the day after the feeding of the 5000, and centre on Jesus' relationship with Moses and the law. In the feeding of the 5000, Jesus called to mind the manna by which the people of Israel were sustained each day in the wilderness. The people credit Moses with providing the gift of manna in the past, but Jesus tells them that it is God the Father who gives the true bread in the present (6:32). In fact, the bread of God is 'that which comes down from heaven and gives life to the world' (v. 33).

By using the words '*I am* the bread of life', Jesus identifies himself with the manna (v. 35). Humanity does not live by bread alone but by every word that comes from the mouth of the Lord (Deuteronomy 8:3). The true sustaining bread, which the Jewish leaders associated with Moses and the law, is none other than Jesus, the very word of God. He is the one who gives life to the world, for he is the bread of life (vv. 35, 41, 48). Just as the Israelites depended on the manna in the wilderness, our daily sustenance as disciples of Jesus depends on the food of his body and blood, given for us on the cross (v. 53). We live because he died (vv. 54–57). It is this that we remember with thankfulness whenever we come to the Lord's Supper.

The fact that bread is also linked with the Torah (law) suggests that our sustenance as disciples also depends on being nurtured as we encounter Jesus in the scriptures.

5 Then you will know

John 8:21–30

In the Gospel of John, Jesus often uses the words 'I am…' to apply a biblical image to himself to speak about his role. In John 8, his discourse begins with his claim to be the light of the world (v. 12). Jesus fulfils Isaiah's prophecy that a light would arise from Galilee (Isaiah 9:1–2; compare John 7:52) and is probably also taking up his reference to the Lord's servant as a light to the Gentiles (Isaiah 42:6). Yet these sayings linked with an image are not the only 'I am' sayings. There are also at least six sayings without an image (4:26; 6:20; 8:24, 28, 58; 13:19), which speak more about Jesus' identity and his identification with the Father. In today's reading we have two of these sayings (vv. 24, 28), which are explicitly linked to Jesus being 'lifted up' on the cross.

Throughout John 8, there are are echoes of Isaiah 42 and 43, where the Lord sets his case before the gods of the nations. There, God, the creator of the world, appoints his servant Israel to be a light for the nations, to open the eyes of those who are blind (42:6–7). This is echoed not only in the saying of John 8:12, but also in the opening of the eyes of the man born blind in John 9. Then, in Isaiah 43:10 the Lord speaks of a day when the people of Israel will 'know and believe me and understand that I am he'. These words are almost exactly mirrored in the two 'I am' sayings of John 8:24 and 28. Jesus takes words that Isaiah used to refer to the exclusive claim of God to be the Saviour (Isaiah 43:11) and applies them to himself. Jesus tells his hearers to believe (v. 24) that 'I am he' so that they will not die in their sins. When they lift him up, they will also know that 'I am he' (v. 28).

Here Jesus offers a way out of sin and its consequences—to believe that 'I am he'. He also offers knowledge of who he really is. It is on the cross that we see most clearly that Jesus is identified with the words, the salvation and even the very nature of God (vv. 28–29).

6 It is better for one man to die

The resurrection of Lazarus (John 11:1–44) forms the climax of Jesus' public ministry. Here the disciples see the glory of God demonstrated spectacularly as Jesus claims to be the resurrection and the life (v. 25) and then proves his claim by raising his friend from the grave (v. 44).

We might expect Jesus' opponents finally to recognise his right to make these audacious claims about his relationship with God. Instead, however, they regard the raising of Lazarus as a threat (v. 48), and the miracle becomes the catalyst for their decision to put Jesus to death (v. 53). John records the words of the high priest Caiaphas. At one level, Caiaphas' statement appears to be an expression of expedient politics that regard the life of one person as expendable to ensure that the status quo is not upset. For the sake of one individual, the Jewish leaders could not afford to upset the uneasy peace with the Romans. Yet John tells us that Caiaphas' words were prophetic, signifying that Jesus would die 'for' the nation and indeed for the whole world (vv. 51–52). Here we have the irony that the counterplot of the story (the attempt to save the nation from political calamity by getting rid of Jesus) actually brings about the main plot of the story (in which Jesus' death saves the nation and the world from an even greater calamity). So Caiaphas tells us more about the significance of Jesus' death than he ever intended.

Again there are echoes from the Old Testament. The sacrificial system was understood in terms of something dying 'for' someone else. The Passover lamb was sacrificed so that the people of Israel would not die. The high priest sacrificed animals 'for' the people, especially on the Day of Atonement. While substitutionary sacrifice may be an unpopular concept in our day, it forms part of the worldview of the Hebrew Bible, where sacrifice was made 'for' the sins of the nation (see, for example, Leviticus 16:15–16). Isaiah 53 also speaks of God's servant suffering and dying on behalf of the iniquities and transgression of his people (vv. 5, 8). In John's story, this Old Testament background transforms Caiaphas' statement of political expediency into the theological key to understanding Jesus' death. It is indeed better for one person to die for the people than that the whole nation should perish.

Guidelines

In the stories that we have read from the first half of the Gospel of John, we have heard constant echoes of the Old Testament. We have also seen how Jesus' impending death is foreshadowed throughout his life. John presents us with three lenses that all interpret one another. We cannot understand Jesus without the Old Testament or the cross. We cannot understand the Old Testament without the cross or Jesus. We cannot understand the cross without Jesus or the Old Testament. For John, these three lenses constantly interplay. As if in a telescope, they focus the light to magnify the significance of what we see in the story of Jesus.

Here is the challenge to our discipleship and our learning. Despite all the complexities of the Old Testament narrative and the history of God's dealings with the people of Israel, John suggests that it is here that we find the key to understanding Jesus. Despite all the pain and shame of the cross, John suggests that it is here that we find God revealed to us in all his love and glory. John implies that we need to wrestle with the Old Testament scriptures and the countercultural mystery of God's glory revealed in the shame of the cross, if we are to understand Jesus and what it means to say that he is the Messiah and the Son of God (20:31–32). Yet this struggle is not just an intellectual exercise. As we come to understand and believe in such a Jesus, John promises that we will find life in his name. It is in this Jesus, who fulfils the role of the shepherd promised in Ezekiel 34 and 37 by laying down his life for the sheep, that we can experience the fullness of life (John 10:10).

1 Countercultural leadership

John 13:1–20

Here we have a remarkable story. John sets up the episode by describing the extraordinary knowledge of Jesus—knowledge of his impending departure to the Father (v. 1) and knowledge that the Father has given everything into his hands (v. 3). How will Jesus use such knowledge? Will he demonstrate the power invested in him by the Father as the culture of his day might expect? No. Instead, he does what no other 'lord' or 'teacher' in the ancient world has ever done: he takes a towel, pours water into a basin and begins to wash the disciples' feet. Just as baptism would symbolise the complete washing that Jesus offers through the cross (vv. 9–10), the foot-washing is a symbol of the daily cleansing that Jesus offers to his disciples from the grime of living in the world.

More than that, this is a symbol of the countercultural nature of the cross. Jesus is taking upon himself a task that he should not be doing in order to serve those he loves. When we read this in the light of the rest of the New Testament, we hear echoes of Mark 10:45 and Philippians 2, echoes that speak of Jesus' countercultural mission of humble service to humanity, taking on the role of a slave coming into this world not to be served but to serve. This humility is seen not only in the incarnation but ultimately in Jesus' self-sacrificial death (Philippians 2:7–8), a death that involved the shame and humiliation of crucifixion, usually reserved for criminals and slaves.

Just as Paul presents Jesus' humility as an example, so the foot-washing is an example for the disciples to emulate. Some churches take it as a command to be followed literally in their worship services. Whatever we think about this, the command to follow the example of humble service for one another could not be put more emphatically (vv. 13–15). If God has placed us in any position of responsibility, are we going to use it in the way that our culture expects, to serve our own ends, or are we going to follow the countercultural example of Jesus in a service of self-sacrifice?

2 What is truth?

John 18:28–38a

In his prologue, John introduced us to the Word made flesh in whom we see 'grace and truth' (vv. 14, 17), the loving-kindness and faithfulness of the God of the Hebrew scriptures. As the Gospel unfolds, 'truth' and its associated terms develop their meaning in relation to Jesus. The true light that was coming into the world (1:9) attracts to himself whoever does what is true (3:21). The hour is coming when true worshippers will worship in 'spirit and truth' (4:23–24). The 'true bread' is not what Moses gave in the wilderness but what the Father gives from heaven (6:32, 35). Jesus' testimony about himself and his relationship with the Father is true (8:14–18) and, ultimately, Jesus is the truth (14:6).

Now we observe Jesus' trial before Pilate. The accusation against Jesus is that he claims to be 'king of the Jews' (v. 33). If found guilty, he should be executed for insurrection but there is a complication. Rather than setting up a kingdom in opposition to Rome (v. 36), Jesus claims to have come to 'bear witness to the truth' (v. 37).

When the Roman governor asks 'What is truth?' (v. 38) he is saying something far more significant than he intends (as so often happens in John: see also 4:25–26; 6:30–32; 11:50–52). Pilate, the judge, should be the one who is able to discern the truth. As Jesus is tried, we are forced to ask: who is on trial? We already know that the Father has given Jesus the authority not only to be a witness (8:18) but to execute judgement (5:27). When Pilate asks, 'What is truth?' we know that the one with whom he speaks *is* the answer, and we know that Pilate will actually be judged by the way he answers his own question. If he recognises Jesus as the truth, he will not come under judgement but will pass from death to life (5:24).

Through Pilate, John asks the same question of his readers: 'What is truth?' As we observe Jesus' trial, we too are tried. According to John, the way we respond to Pilate's question has eternal consequences.

3 Shall I crucify your king?

John 18:38b—19:16

The trial scene continues. As we noted yesterday, the charge is that Jesus has illegitimately set himself up as a king. The trial is full of irony. As readers of the Gospel, we have known Jesus' identity as the 'king of Israel' from the very first chapter, when Nathaniel first recognised him as such (1:49). The theme of kingship has echoed through the story, coming to prominence after the feeding of the 5000, where Jesus resisted the crowd's attempt to make him king by force (6:15). It recurred in Jesus' claim to be the good shepherd, as he contrasted himself with the hired hands (10:13–14). There, he assumed the role of shepherd prophesied by Ezekiel 34:23–24 in contrast to the leaders who had not cared for God's flock (34:2–6). Again the theme came to the fore in the triumphal entry (John 12:15), with its resonances of Zechariah 9:9: 'Lo, your king comes to you…'

With this knowledge in our minds, we read the story of Jesus' trial, where Pilate publicly declares that Jesus is the King of the Jews (19:14). The soldiers sarcastically dress Jesus up as king (vv. 1–3), while Pilate goes in and out of the praetorium asking questions of the Jewish leaders and of Jesus alternately. Some commentators suggest that rather than being manipulated by the crowd, Pilate is manipulating them, forcing them to declare their allegiance to Rome. Others suggest that Pilate himself is scared of the consequences of his decision (see v. 8). Whatever we conclude, the Jewish leaders, backed by the crowd, consistently reject Jesus as their king until they emphatically declare allegiance to Caesar as their only king (v. 15) and Pilate hands Jesus over to be crucified.

That is not the end. The argument continues into the following section, for Pilate writes a sign in Aramaic, Latin and Greek, which he refuses to change: 'What I have written I have written' (v. 22). On the cross, Jesus is declared to be king in the languages of the Jews, the Roman empire and whole Greek world. Here, in this most cruel form of execution, John emphasises the fulfilment of all that his story has been about. The irony is that, in his rejection as king by his own people, Jesus is declared to be king to the whole world.

4 Behold, the Lamb of God (2)

John 19:16–37

'None of his bones shall be broken' (v. 36). John tells us that these words were fulfilled when Jesus died before the soldiers could break his legs (v. 33). The significance is not just in their literal fulfilment but in all that these few words imply. By quoting Exodus 12:46, John brings to mind the Passover festival, during which each family would eat a lamb in their own home in remembrance of the day when the Lord brought the people of Israel out of the land of Egypt (Exodus 12:51).

John records three Passover festivals in which he links Jesus' death to the Passover and the exodus where God saved his people from slavery. The first occurs in John 2:13, where Jesus clears the money-changers out of the temple and declares that he will destroy the temple and raise it again in three days (2:19). John links this explicitly to Jesus' death and resurrection. The second Passover occurs around the time when Jesus feeds the 5000 (6:4), an incident that echoes Moses and the Israelites in the wilderness. We have already seen how this sign, along with Jesus' claim to be the bread of life, was linked to his death. In the build-up to Jesus' death, the third Passover has been highlighted several times (12:1; 13:1; 18:28).

As Jesus dies, John informs us that it is the day of Preparation for the Passover (19:14, 31). In view of the links between Jesus' death and this feast, the quotation from Exodus 12:46 indicates that the reason Jesus' bones are not broken is that he has become the Passover lamb. In his death a new and greater deliverance is taking place. John further explains the significance of Jesus' death in terms of Zechariah's prophecy about a day when the inhabitants of Jerusalem will 'look on the one whom they have pierced' and mourn 'as one mourns for an only child' (Zechariah 12:10). The result of that day of mourning is that a fountain is opened for the house of David and the inhabitants of Jerusalem 'to cleanse them from sin and impurity' (Zechariah 13:1). The Passover Lamb is 'lifted up' so that they will experience this greater salvation and will not die in their sins (John 8:24).

5 I have seen the Lord

John 20:1–18

'Seeing' is one of John's great themes. In 1:14, he declares that we have seen Jesus' glory. John the Baptist sees Jesus and declares him to be the Lamb of God (1:29, 36). Philip encourages the sceptical Nathaniel to come and see Jesus for himself (1:46). As we read the Gospel, seeing becomes a symbol for understanding who Jesus is. Ironically, the Pharisees can literally see but they are metaphorically blind, while the man who was born blind sees, understands and even worships Jesus (9:35–

41). The disciples struggle to see, so Jesus has to explain that 'whoever has seen me has seen the Father' (14:9).

As John's Gospel draws to its conclusion, the resurrection becomes the key to understanding all that has gone before. It is the lens through which Jesus' ministry and death make sense (see 2:22). Like a piece of music, the mood changes from a minor to a major key and everything brightens. Themes clashing with disharmony in Jesus' crucifixion now interweave in a surprising harmony. The dissonance is resolved, first in the story of Mary that we have read today, then in the stories of the other disciples (20:19–23) and finally in the story of doubting Thomas (20:24–29).

In her encounter on that resurrection morning, Mary's tearful eyes are opened as she hears Jesus call her by name (v. 16). Mary refers to Jesus as 'my Lord' (v. 13), 'Sir' (v. 15), 'Rabbouni' (v. 16) and finally 'the Lord' (v. 18). The word 'lord' can be used of a master or as a term of respect. It is also used to translate the name of God in the Greek Old Testament. After the resurrection, the church quickly adopted it to refer to Jesus. Mary is the first of the post-resurrection disciples to ascribe this title to Jesus. She has not only physically seen the risen Jesus; she has also recognised him as 'the Lord' who will soon be worshipped by Thomas and believed in by many who have not seen (20:28–29). These things are also written so that *we* may believe that Jesus is the Christ, the Son of God, and that we may have eternal life in his name (vv. 30–31).

6 From failed disciple to faithful follower

John 21

Coming as an epilogue to John's Gospel, Jesus' encounter with the disciples on the shore of Galilee has often been called into question. Whether this passage was originally part of John's story of Jesus or was added later, its location on the shores of Lake Galilee is significant. It carries echoes of other Gospel stories—echoes of the calling of the fisherman disciples (Mark 1:16–20), the stilling of the sea (Mark 4:35–41), the walking on the water (Mark 6:45–51), the feeding of the 5000 (John 6:1–15) and, most of all, echoes of the miraculous catch of fish (Luke 5:1–11).

In John, this story takes on an important post-resurrection significance. What will happen to Peter, the disciple whom all the Gospels have identified as a failure because of his denial of Jesus? In a wonderful ending to the Gospel, all such disciples are given hope as they witness Jesus' gentle restoration of Peter to discipleship and his commissioning to take care of the flock. In an echo of Peter's threefold denial, Jesus asks Peter three times, 'Do you love me?' (vv. 15–17). Despite his shame and hurt, Peter responds positively to each question and, in reply, Jesus commissions him. Peter the failure seems particularly suited to caring for the needs of the sheep, and his restoration gives him a ministry that he would perhaps have been unsuited for if he had never known what it was to deny Jesus. Here is the grace of the gospel, that Jesus is able to restore us and use us, not only despite our failings and our weaknesses but actually because of them. This is a lesson that Paul also learnt the hard way (2 Corinthians 4:7–12; 12:8–10).

As the shepherd of God's flock, Peter has one more temptation—to look over his shoulder and worry about the ministry that Jesus has entrusted to the beloved disciple (vv. 20–23). That is none of his concern. He is simply to follow Jesus (vv. 20, 24). As those restored by Jesus' grace, here is the challenge to us—to follow Jesus and not to worry about what he has called our neighbour to do.

Guidelines

The passages we have studied this week continually challenge our worldview. The washing of the disciples' feet confronts our understanding of authority and power as Jesus sets us an example of humble service of others. Jesus' trial calls us to redefine truth, not simply in terms of the factual, the scientific or even the weighing of evidence in court, but in terms of Jesus' testimony to God's character and his demonstration of God's love. In Jesus' discussion with Pilate, we have been challenged by a kingship that supersedes the kingdoms and confronts the political powers of this world. In Jesus' death as the Passover Lamb, God acts to bring about a great deliverance through the most shameful form of criminal execution that the ancient world could offer. Then, as the resurrection morning dawns, we discover that there is hope in the darkest of places. When we, like Mary, feel lost, insignificant and confused, the risen Lord Jesus calls us by name. Finally, there is even hope in our failures and weaknesses, for the Lord Jesus does not commission those who are perfect but those who have failed and yet experienced forgiveness.

In all these stories, John challenges us to think differently from the world around us and to act in the light of a worldview that he describes as coming 'from above' rather than our daily worldview that is shaped 'from below'. But how can we see the world from this heavenly perspective when the ideologies of our own society are so strong and persuasive? Partly, as we observe Jesus in the light of the Old Testament and the cross, but also as we, with Thomas in the upper room and the disciples on the lake, encounter the risen Lord Jesus in our daily lives and respond to him in adoration, worship and commitment (20:27–28). In entrusting ourselves to the countercultural message of the risen Lord Jesus, we begin to see our world 'from above'. As we do this, John encourages us with the assurance that we will receive a blessing from Jesus because we have believed in him even though we have not seen him (20:29).

FURTHER READING

J.C. Ryle, *John: Expository Thoughts* Vols 1 and 2, Banner of Truth, 1987.

William Temple, *Readings in St John's Gospel*, Morehouse, 1985.

C.J.H. Wright, *Knowing Jesus through the Old Testament*, IVP, 1995.

Ruth

Goethe described the book of Ruth as 'the loveliest little piece... among the epics and idylls of the past', but for Thomas Paine, a political activist of the 18th century, Ruth was a futile story 'about a strolling country girl, creeping slyly to bed with her cousin Boaz'.

Both the 'romantic' and the 'worthless' assessments fail to acknowledge how provocative Ruth's context is. Behind the details of peasant life, a genetic connection is being established between the most important royal figure (King David) and the Moabite bloodline, at a time when the exclusion of the Moabites from the Lord's people (Deuteronomy 23:3) would have been fresh in the reader's mind.

If we are to accept a post-exilic date for the writing of the book, based on linguistic arguments, then Ruth is set in contrast to the theology of ethnic purity found in Ezra and Nehemiah. This makes Ruth a subversive book, which, like Job, wrestles with a particular theological position of its time.

The various positions that the book of Ruth is given in the canon of scripture affect the way it is approached today. Our English Bibles place it between Judges and 1 Samuel. In doing so, they follow the Septuagint and Vulgate, which consider Ruth to be a prelude to the history of the Davidic dynasty. However, the Masoretic text (the traditional Jewish text of the Old Testament) lists Ruth as part of the 'Writings', following immediately after Proverbs' description of the ideal woman (*'eshet hayil*). This sets Ruth, the woman, in parallel to this figure—a theme that is put centre-stage in many feminist interpretations. In Jewish liturgy, Ruth is read during the feast of Pentecost (*Shevuot*), when the giving of the Torah is also celebrated. Later rabbinic sources point to Ruth as the key example of how to understand and apply the relation between the letter of the Law and the spirit in which it should be kept.

Permeating all these readings is the theme of *hesed*, a word that is often translated as 'loving-kindness' but carries a wider meaning of benevolence and faithfulness. In Ruth, *hesed* is present in the actions of each protagonist who goes beyond what is legally required. It is through the expression of *hesed* that the law provides redemption, a pagan woman becomes part of God's people and a son is born—themes that will culminate in the person and ministry of Christ, the descendant and ultimate fulfilment of this union.

1 Setting the scene

Ruth 1:1–6

Regardless of the date of the writing, the story is clearly set during the time of Judges. This was a time of recurring apostasy, judgement and salvation. Some commentators see the perils of this period (for example, Judges 19–20; 21:25) as the background against which the drama of two women is played. Others understand the opening Hebrew expression 'when judges *were judging*' as referring to a safer time.

The beginning of the story follows a chiastic structure, setting in parallel famine (v. 1) and food (v. 6b), leaving (v. 2) and returning (v. 6a), husband's death (v. 3) and children's deaths (v. 5). At the centre of the structure stands the marriage of Naomi's sons with the Moabites (v. 4).

The region of Moab was around 50 miles south-east of Bethlehem, beyond the Dead Sea, the southern part of what today is Jordan. Biblical accounts give a negative portrayal of Moab the man and his descendants. He was born as a result of incest between Lot and his elder daughter (Genesis 19:36–37). A Moabite king tried to curse Israel using Balaam (Numbers 22), and Moabite women led Israel into idolatry (Numbers 25). Thus, Moabites were seen as enemies, and friendship with them was strictly forbidden in Israel (Deuteronomy 23:3–6). The implications of all this for Naomi's daughters-in-law would have not been missed by the original readers, and the author makes sure the point is not forgotten by referring to Ruth continuously and, it might seem, unnecessarily as 'the Moabite' (1:4, 22; 2:2, 6, 21; 4:5).

Nevertheless, the author introduces this detail without passing any judgement, in contrast to Ezra (9:1–4). In fact, in verse 2 he seems to hint subtly at acceptance, by referring, amid a series of family and geographic names, to the origin of the family as 'Ephrathites from Bethlehem'. As well as the thematic wordplay about famine in the 'house of bread' (*Beth-lehem*), the first readers would have immediately spotted an echo of David's origin: he is described specifically as the 'son of an Ephrathite of Bethlehem' in 1 Samuel 17:12. The same location would become the symbol of the messianic promise in Micah 5:2.

When Ruth is read as part of the series about the great judges, we cannot fail to notice the contrast with the tumult and strife of that time period. Yet, it is within the 'battle' of the social relationships of two child-less widows, and not in the context of mighty military heroes, that God starts to unveil his lasting rescue plan of a Messiah.

2 Return

Ruth 1:7–22

William Blake captures the drama of this passage in his painting *Naomi Entreating Ruth and Orpah to Return to the Land of Moab*, where Ruth clings to Naomi, who is portrayed as a Christ-like figure, while Orpah departs lamenting. The biblical text is infused with raw emotion, displayed in four dialogues that are interwoven with short emotive remarks about kisses, weeping and agitation. All the dialogues follow the theme of return, towards either Judah or Moab. Each one is packed with thematic and theological implications—for example, Naomi's appeal to the *hesed* of God and of her daughters-in-law, similarities with the Judah and Tamar story, and a Job-like lamentation in the face of agitated observers. We will focus on the third dialogue (vv. 15–17), which is seen as key to the whole book.

This dialogue is often understood as Ruth's religious and social conversion, which would resolve the Moabite issue. However, the conversion doesn't 'naturalise' Ruth. She is still continually described as 'the Moabite'. Whether we think the author does this to challenge the reader or to reflect the unfinished process of Ruth's conversion depends on how we understand the nature of her commitment.

Ruth's speech resembles the kind of covenant oaths found in 2 Samuel 15:19–21 and 1 Kings 22:4. There are also elements of proselytism, following in the line of Targum to Ruth, in which rabbinic interpretation expands the text, setting Ruth's fourfold statement as a response to the questions of whether she will observe the sabbath, avoid lodging with non-Jewish people, keep all the commandments and worship no idols. It is clear, however, that her turning towards Israel and Yahweh results from her loving-kindness towards Naomi and not vice versa.

Ruth's loving-kindness is sacrificial and goes beyond what was legally required. She clings to the fate of a childless widow, to a people who see her as an enemy and to a God who seems to have turned against Naomi (v. 13). In this, Ruth's commitment seems to surpass even Abraham's decision to leave his country and kindred, as Phyllis Trible observes:

Ruth stands alone; she possesses nothing. No God has called her; no deity has promised her blessing; no human being has come to her aid. She lives and chooses without a support group and she knows that the fruit of her decision may well be the emptiness of rejection, indeed of death. (God and the Rhetoric of Sexuality, p. 173).

Perhaps Blake's portrayal of Ruth clinging to a Christ-like figure resonates with the clinging of the women at the foot of the cross. Like the meaning of Naomi's new name, Mara (v. 20), their devotion was in the face of bitterness, the Lord's judgement and a lack of future hope—a loving-kindness that challenges us even today.

3 Gleaning

Ruth 2

This chapter is constructed of five dialogues, set in a chiastic structure with a certain amount of editorial work between them:

Ruth — Naomi (v. 2)
    Boaz — reapers (vv. 4–7)
        Boaz — Ruth (vv. 8–14)
    Boaz — reapers (vv. 15–16)
Naomi — Ruth (vv. 19–22)

Boaz is the key protagonist, introduced in verse 1 as 'a mighty man of power' ('ish gibor hayil). The term can apply to a military leader or any wealthy or honorable person, and this has provided room for rabbinic speculation to identify Boaz as one of the judges, perhaps Ibzan (Judges 12:8–10).

Ruth, too, takes centre-stage while Naomi fades into the background. She is portrayed as taking initiative and being a hard worker, grateful and obedient. Her reputation is commented on in 3:11, where she is described as a 'worthy woman' (*'eshet hayil*), a similar description to the one given to Boaz. Some commentators see this as a reference to Ruth's affluent Moabite origin, others to her character.

The encounter between Ruth and Boaz is at the heart of the chapter. The social context is that of gleaning, an activity by which needy people, according to the law, were allowed to collect any grain left behind by the reapers. Boaz's actions, however, go beyond what the law required. He provides protection, food and direct access to the fields. His benevolence is the answer to Ruth's loving-kindness towards Naomi and her people, which Boaz describes in similar vocabulary as is used for God's call to Abraham to leave his land and family (v. 11; see Genesis 12:1). Ruth's commitment to God is expressed indirectly through the blessing that Boaz gives her (v. 12).

Boaz's motive for using this style of speech has been the subject of many contradictory interpretations. In my opinion, the use of a blessing serves to elevate Ruth's sacrifice to such a point that it cannot be fully rewarded by Boaz's modest benevolence. A medieval rabbi paraphrases Boaz's reply: 'God alone can adequately reward you for your acts of *hesed*.' Ruth's sacrificial loving-kindness cannot be rewarded with just 20–40 kilogrammes of barley, despite the fact that this was a large amount for a day's work.

The content of the blessing changes the medium through which the Moabite issue is raised. The question 'What will God's reward look like for such loving-kindness?' would have agitated the mind of a post-exilic reader who might have been overly concerned with the question 'What does God's judgement look like for the past sins of the Moabites?'

4 Encounter

Ruth 3

It seems hard to fully capture the characters' motives and the cultural background in chapter 3. This has led to a variety of speculations from both ancient and modern interpreters. The secrecy element, laden with sexual overtones, seems to make the story too risqué. Perhaps the author chooses this path on purpose, to allude to and redeem the scandalous stories of the protagonists' ancestors (Lot's incest with his daughters, and Judah's relationship with Tamar, in Genesis 19:30–38 and 38:12–30 respectively).

Naomi's desire to provide security for Ruth echoes her initial blessing in 1:9. However, here it is not a mere wish but a concrete plan. She has become the agent through which her blessing will be fulfilled. Naomi's continuing advice to Ruth highlights a contrast with Judah. Like Naomi, he was at first unable to provide a levirate husband for his foreign daughter-in-law, Tamar. However, whereas Judah refused to fulfil his responsibility to Tamar when his young son came of age, Naomi goes beyond what she can physically provide.

Boaz also goes beyond the legal requirements and, in doing so, he too becomes the agent of his own blessing. 'The wings of the Lord' (*kenafaim*, singular *kanaf*), under which Ruth took refuge in 2:12, now materialise into Boaz's robe (*kanaf*) that is spread over her (3:9). Similar imagery is found in Ezekiel 16:8, where it refers to the symbolic marriage of Yahweh with Israel.

Ruth's actions are also set in contrast to the behaviour of Tamar and of Lot's daughters. While they covered their identities, with the help of clothing and alcohol respectively, Ruth clearly shows her identity and her intention for marriage. In the light of 2 Samuel 12:20, the change in her appearance (v. 3) should not be seen as a seduction technique but as a sign that she is distancing herself from the mourning required of a widow. There is, however, an ambiguity in the act of 'uncovering feet' (vv. 4, 7). Some scholars see this as a euphemism for a sexual act, referring either to Boaz's sexual organs (compare Exodus 4:25) or to Ruth undressing at his feet, but the portrayal of Boaz as an honourable man throughout the book and his comments after the encounter suggest the opposite of a scandal. So, why the secrecy? It seems from Boaz's surprised reaction that he might have not been the most natural choice for Ruth, either because of his age or because there was another relative in line. Naomi's initiative might have backfired, resulting in a replay of their ancestral scandals.

5 Marriage

The socio-legal aspects of this passage, concerning the redeemer and the levir, have raised many questions. The role of a redeemer is to pay back the cost of land (or a person) that has been sold, whereas a levir (the English form comes from the Latin meaning 'brother-in-law') is a man who is obliged to marry his widowed sister-in-law. According to the Pentateuch, these are two separate roles. Boaz has already been described in previous chapters as a redeemer, but his main argument in these negotiations seems to presuppose a levirate role.

The textual problems in verse 5 add to the ambiguity. The original written form (the actual Hebrew consonants) puts the second occurrence of the verb 'acquire' in the first person, as if Boaz is referring to himself ('When you acquire the land, I acquire Ruth), a model followed by the Revised English Bible. The marginal vowel corrections found in the Masoretic text, however, allow the verb to be pronounced in the second person, as if it refers to the relative ('When you acquire the land, you acquire Ruth). If the original form is followed, then Boaz's argument is not based on the levirate duty. He himself will marry Ruth without any obligation to do so. The risk for the relative, then, will be a descendant from this marriage who will claim back the property and make his investment worthless. This is the line that Ibn Ezra and some modern scholars follow, but the discussion is ongoing.

Among all these details, it is important to notice the role of the community. All the legal arrangements take place at the gate of the city, in front of the elders. The Moabite issue is not just a family matter any more, but is open to the entire community. However, the question at hand is presented from the perspective of a redeemer's responsibility. There is no mention of Ruth's credentials (for example, her conversion or her sacrificial loving-kindness), apart from her widowed status and the need to keep the name of the family alive. Some see this as Boaz's genius in finding a legal 'loophole'.

The community gives approval through a blessing that puts Ruth among the matriarchs of God's people. The reasons for this approval are not elaborated, but the unusual reference to Tamar and Judah could be seen as the motive. The contrast between these two stories, already hinted at in the last chapter, could mean that the same reasons for accepting the descendant of Tamar and Judah would be applied, even more so, to the descendant of Boaz and Ruth.

6 A son is born

Ruth 4:13–18

For the first time, the author introduces the Lord as a key protagonist in the story. So far he has been mentioned only to set the scene (1:6) or, indirectly, in the words of a blessing. There has been no divine comment during the development of the story. In claiming God's intervention in Ruth's pregnancy, the author now brings divine approval to the marriage.

The birth of the son brings a reversal of Naomi's ordeal described in the first chapter. The townspeople's agitation is turned into the women's blessing; God's 'bitter' act towards Naomi has been transformed into a life-giving event; her Moabite daughter-in-law is valued more than seven sons. It is interesting that Naomi, not Ruth or Boaz, is the object of this blessing. Even the name of the son, meaning 'one who serves', seems to be linked with the service made to Naomi in rekindling her life and bringing nourishment. This has led some scholars to conclude that Ruth's identity remained unresolved: she was accepted only as a surrogate mother. However, when the chapter is read in its totality, it becomes obvious that the author is addressing all three protagonists—Ruth at the gate, Naomi among the women and Boaz in the genealogy of David.

The messianic conclusion brings a final approval to the union between Ruth and Boaz. The Moabite ancestry of David is not mentioned elsewhere in the Old Testament. It could explain, however, the good relationship that David had with the king of Moab, to whom he entrusted his parents in 1 Samuel 22:1–4.

The messianic conclusion also brings another dimension to the theme of the redeemer, which until now has been played out only within a family and legal context. As the book of Ruth makes the transition between the period of the Judges and the Davidic dynasty, the blessings given to Ruth and Naomi capture the hope of the entire nation. The same messianic theme is picked up in Matthew's genealogy of Christ (Matthew 1:1–16), where it is expanded to include some of the female characters. Ruth is mentioned there alongside Tamar and Rahab, all women with controversial histories. Matthew 1:5 also cites Rahab as the mother of Boaz. This brings a fascinating interpretative element to the motives behind Boaz's loving-kindness towards Ruth. The inclusion of a Moabite in Christ's genealogy then sets the agenda of the New Testament, where 'there is no longer Jew or Greek… male and female… in Christ Jesus' (Galatians 3:28).

Guidelines

'Ruth,' says the Midrash, 'tells us nothing of ritual purity or defilement, of prohibition or permission. For what purpose was it written? To teach you how great is the reward of those who dispense *hesed*.' The theme of loving-kindness in Ruth is not just another example of how to accept people on the margins. It is the lens through which the entire Law is being interpreted. LaCocque points to this by commenting on the reasons why Ruth is read during the feast of receiving the law: 'For it is not the liturgical use of Ruth during the Feast of *Shevuot* that drove the legal reading of the book, but its contents that drove its connection to the celebration of the gift of the Torah.'

The same theme of interpreting the law in the spirit of loving-kindness is at the heart of the ongoing debates between Jesus and the Pharisees (Matthew 12:7–8). As we dig deeper into the socio-legal context of the challenges present in Ruth and the Gospels, we find that, like today's challenges, they are not simple. Often they bring face to face aspects of the law that seem to be opposites. The thin line between compromise and loving-kindness was a real challenge for the authors of Ruth and the Gospels. For us, giving up on this struggle would be going against the scriptures themselves, and the reward for getting it right is immense. In the context of Ruth, it made real the future vision of Isaiah 56:1–8 and the messianic hope.

Another important aspect is God's involvement in human activity. God seems a distant player, as he does in the book of Esther. He is present mostly in people's blessings, which appear in every chapter, and the entire theology of the book can be deduced by tracing the progression of those blessings. However, as Frymer-Kensky observes, 'The characters in the Book of Ruth themselves act to fulfil the blessing that they bestow on one another in God's name.' To invoke God's presence while becoming this presence for others is the challenge that Ruth's story sets in front of us. The loving-kindness of our human bonds should be the place where God's loving-kindness is found.

Think about our current ethical issues. How would this biblical concept of loving-kindness shape our interpretation of them? Reflect on how becoming God's presence for others should shape our relationships with those close to us and with people on the margins.

FURTHER READING

Frederic Bush, *Ruth, Esther* (Word Biblical Commentary), Thomas Nelson, 1996.

Tamara Cohn Eskanazi and Tikva Frymer-Kensky, *The JPS Bible Commentary: Ruth*, Jewish Publication Society, 2011.

André LaCocque, *A Continental Commentary: Ruth*, Fortress Press, 2004.

Phyllis Trible, *God and the Rhetoric of Sexuality*, Fortress, 1978.

1 Corinthians

In today's world, we often find ourselves overhearing other people's conversations. This can be interesting, irritating or tantalising—particularly when it's a phone conversation and you can only hear one of the two parties involved. Reading Paul's letters to the Corinthians can feel like that: we are listening in on a conversation from long ago, and we can only hear one of the voices. We have to use our imagination when reading Paul's words, to help us fill in the gaps and work out the other side of the conversation—what Paul was hearing from Corinth.

In his travels through Greece, Paul arrived at Corinth in about AD50. He spent a year and a half there, preaching and establishing a church, before moving on to Ephesus (see Acts 18:1–19). While at Ephesus, Paul heard of problems in the Corinthian church; he wrote a letter, warning about the dangers of immorality. This letter, mentioned in 1 Corinthians 5:9, is now lost (unless, as some suggest, it was preserved in what we now call 2 Corinthians 6:14—7:1). Later, around AD54, Paul heard from some Corinthian visitors about divisions in the church and received a letter with questions from Corinth (see 1 Corinthians 1:11; 7:1). In response, Paul wrote the letter that we call 1 Corinthians. The conversation continued, with more visits and further letters, including 2 Corinthians.

Those who become Christians are always people who have been shaped by their culture, for better or worse. The Corinthians lived in a thriving city that prospered because of its location on international trade routes, deriving much wealth from commerce and manufacturing. Every two years, Corinth hosted the famous Isthmian games, where crowds of visitors witnessed contests in sports, music and poetry. As a favoured colony of Rome, the city's security was guaranteed. Competitiveness, self-promotion and success were all part of the pervading ethos of Corinthian life, along with self-sufficiency and reverence for freedom, wisdom and knowledge. Many who responded to the gospel and joined the church brought this kind of mindset with them, with consequences that were sometimes destructive. Like many pastors down the years, Paul sensed an urgent need to help new believers develop different ways of thinking and living. That agenda, evident in this letter, remains highly relevant today.

Biblical quotations are a mixture of NRSV and Anthony Thiselton's translation (from his shorter commentary).

1 Encouraging and confronting

1 Corinthians 1:1–17

Which voice(s) do we hear in 1 Corinthians? Paul mentions himself and Sosthenes (v. 1). The latter could be the Jewish synagogue leader mentioned in Acts 18:17, if he later became a Christian, or he might be the scribe writing down Paul's words (see 16:21, where Paul signs the finished letter himself). Either way, it is Paul's voice that comes through clearly in this letter. As an 'apostle', he is a divinely appointed witness to Christ.

Before launching into his concerns, Paul takes time to give thanks for all that is good in the Corinthian church (vv. 4–9). It was conventional for a letter writer to begin with thanks for some benefit received, such as safe travel or a gift. Paul follows this convention but changes it, focusing not on what he has received but on what God has given to others: their welfare is his agenda. Beginning with thanks and praise sets a positive, encouraging tone. Before confronting the problems, Paul acknowledges that God is at work in the Corinthian church and can be trusted to continue that work.

Paul's visitors from Corinth have brought disturbing news of quarrels in the church. Paul speaks of *schismata* ('splits', v. 10), suggesting something tearing apart. Different factions have developed, each claiming allegiance to an authority figure. We do not know exactly what they are saying. 'Apollos' and 'Peter' may just be code names that Paul uses for particular leaders in Corinth whom he does not want to embarrass by naming them publically. Alternatively, perhaps one group in Corinth is known as the 'Peter group' because they look to Jesus' close friend Peter as the original authority figure or as the symbol of a strongly Jewish type of Christianity that they favour. Another group, meanwhile, focuses on 'Christ alone', perhaps rejecting all other human authority figures in a hyper-spiritual way. A struggle for power has developed. Christians from the competitive world of Corinth, with its admiration for celebrity figures, were prone to such temptations, as we may be in today's culture. Paul asks rhetorically who was crucified for them (v. 13). Even the finest Christian leaders cannot save them; they need to look to the cross of Christ for salvation and remember their commitment to Christ, which they proclaimed when they were baptised.

2 The power and wisdom of the cross

1 Corinthians 1:18—2:5

Paul continues to point his readers to the saving death of Christ, reminding them of what he preached when he first arrived in Corinth. He proclaimed 'the mystery of God', which was all about 'Jesus Christ, and him crucified' (2:1–2). In this message is a power that saves (1:18).

Paul acknowledges the 'foolishness' of this message. Corinth was a Roman colony; Romans regarded death by crucifixion as disgusting and abhorrent, not to be mentioned in polite society. Such an execution was also repulsive to Jews, even a sign of being cursed (see Galatians 3:13). Paul's proclamation of a crucified Messiah would have shocked and outraged many. No wonder he came in fear and trembling, aware of his own weakness (2:3; compare 2 Corinthians 12:8–10), for the cross turns human ideas upside down. This gospel message, which seems foolish, in fact will prove wiser and stronger than what Corinth and Rome value as knowledge and wisdom.

The Corinthian Christians themselves demonstrate this 'foolish wisdom' of God. They come from a mixture of social backgrounds, ranging from a few who are quite well off to a larger number who are poorer. All have responded to the gospel message: it has a universal appeal and relevance that reaches across different backgrounds and types of people. The challenge is to blend this wonderful mixture of people into a united church. The secret is for each of them to delight not in their own achievements and status, which encourages divisive competition, but in belonging to Christ who has bought (redeemed) them through the cross.

Paul's message was offensive to many, and so was his style of speaking.

Classical orators used rhetoric skilfully to convince people of their arguments, and Paul's own letters are full of carefully crafted and reasoned persuasive speech. But a new style had developed, with rhetoric as a competitive performance designed to gain applause, approval and status. Clever speakers, who could argue persuasively even against reason and truth, became celebrities comparable with the most acclaimed actors and gladiators, according to the ancient historian Plutarch. Some in the church wished that Paul could show such qualities and compete with these professionals, but Paul rejects the foolishness of such so-called wisdom among the debaters of the age (1:20). His stance challenges any preacher who is tempted to manipulate their audience and gain applause and status in the process.

3 Christian 'spirituality'

1 Corinthians 2:6—3:4

'Spirituality' has become a popular word in our day: many people value and seek it but a definition proves elusive. It is sometimes seen as a mysterious quality innate in each person, needing to be developed in order to give us peace and fulfilment.

The Bible does not use the term 'spirituality' but is concerned with matters of the spirit. Some of the Christians in the Corinthian church lay claim to the term 'spiritual', and they understand it in ways drawn from their own culture, which looks for an innate higher capacity in each human being, a soul or 'divine spark' seeking release. Paul affirms the Corinthians' desire to be spiritual but redefines the term: a spiritual Christian is someone directed and transformed by the Holy Spirit. The Holy Spirit comes not from within the person but from beyond them, from God (2:12). This Spirit, who is quite different from 'the spirit of the world', needs to be received as a gift or a guest and must be allowed to work in the believer to develop 'the mind of Christ' (v. 16). The Holy Spirit has intimate access to the depths of God's very being (vv. 10–11) and, therefore, knows secrets and mysteries that can never be discovered simply by human effort and study. Elsewhere Paul does speak of human beings having their own 'spirit' within them; but this spirit needs to be energised, not by self-help but by contact with God the Holy Spirit (see Romans 8:9–11, 16).

Paul has spent time getting to know those to whom he writes. He regularly uses words and catchphrases that are popular among the Corinthian Christians, such as 'spiritual'; other popular terms include 'wisdom', 'knowledge' and 'mature'. True wisdom is not achieved by human effort and cleverness but is revealed by God in the crucified Christ and received as a gift (vv. 7–9).

Paul wants to feed the Corinthians with the 'solid food' of Christian teaching, but they are still not ready for it. Their infantile attention-seeking and quarrelling are signs of immaturity, not of true spirituality (3:1–3). Power games in the church, arising from a childish desire for excessive attention, can be a problem in our time as much as in Paul's. We too need the Holy Spirit to do a deeper work, developing Christ-like minds and attitudes in us.

4 Valuing Christian leaders

1 Corinthians 3:5–17; 4:6–13

As we saw at the start of the letter, the Corinthian Christians are having difficulty developing healthy attitudes to their leaders. To those who seek celebrities to admire, Paul gives a reminder that leaders are simply servants of Christ and the church. On the other hand, to those who claim a personal hotline to heaven and dismiss the need for any recognised leadership, Paul points out that the work done by people like himself and Apollos is a crucial part of God's work in establishing and growing the Corinthian church.

Paul explores three metaphors of the church and its leaders. First, the church is a field, which needs cultivation by wise and hardworking leaders in order to produce a good harvest, which ultimately comes from God (3:6–9). Second, the church can be seen as a building, which needs to be raised up on a firm foundation and must hold together in coherent unity (vv. 9–15). A leader such as Paul is like a managing architect who coordinates a team of builders, keeping an overview of the whole project. They should build something solid that will last, founded on Christ, and the quality of their work will be revealed in God's final judgement. 'Building up' is a significant theme of this letter (see 8:1; 10:23; 14:4). Third, refining the metaphor, Paul sees this building as God's temple, which is above all a holy place, since God's Holy Spirit is present there (vv. 16–17).

After further reflections on the deceptiveness of the world's so-called wisdom (3:18—4:5), Paul reminds the Corinthians of God's grace: 'What do you have that you did not receive?' (4:7). They are not a 'self-made' church: the cross, the preaching of the gospel and the Holy Spirit are all gifts from God. The believers should not boast of their spiritual achievements in a self-congratulatory way, as some religious groups of their time did. To puncture such triumphalism, Paul 'boasts' with biting irony of the struggles and sufferings he has experienced in his ministry (4:9–13), in contrast with the triumphalism of some in Corinth who look for comfort and status. Paul paints a picture of leadership that is demanding and unglamorous, in order to challenge their misconceptions. He confronts their wrong thinking, but does so out of fatherly concern for the welfare of his children (see 4:14–21).

5 Confronting a scandal

1 Corinthians 5

When Paul preached the gospel, he proclaimed freedom—from sin and from the burden of the law (compare Galatians 5:1). Many of the Corinthian Christians warmed to this idea; some developed a new slogan: 'All things are lawful for me' (6:12; 10:23). This distortion of Paul's teaching about freedom caused problems and may have contributed to particular moral issues, which he now addresses.

Paul's visitors have told him of an illicit sexual relationship in the Corinthian congregation, which he condemns as outrageous (v. 1). The complacency of the church about this matter concerns him. Some scholars wonder if a wealthy patron was involved, whom the church did not want to offend by condemning the behaviour; or perhaps the relationship was being used to manipulate inheritance laws to the benefit of the church.

Paul tells the Christians to cut themselves off from the offending man, who is following 'the flesh' (v. 5), a phrase that Paul uses to mean self-sufficient living for one's own purposes, without dependence on God. Paul's call for the man to be expelled may sound harsh to us, but his hope is that, cut off from the approval and support of the church community, the offender will have a change of heart and repent. If the present situation continues to be tolerated, this will not happen.

To help those who wonder why this is such a big deal, Paul turns to the imagery of the Passover festival. Leaven is a tiny substance that has unstoppable effects, out of all proportion to its size (see Matthew 13:33). Similarly, tolerating this one problem may infect the whole church with damaging attitudes, which may then develop into other problems. Just as every speck of old leaven was thrown out at Passover, enabling a new start in the household, so the Christian community is a new creation and needs to express this radical newness by purging aspects of the old life. Like Israel of old, redeemed from Egypt, they are given a new identity and lifestyle (vv. 6–8).

When Paul tells them not to 'associate' with immoral people, and lists other examples (vv. 9–11), the word he uses literally suggests 'mixing up together with'. He is not arguing for total withdrawal into a supposedly pure Christian ghetto, but he is warning against indifference or complacency that blurs distinctive Christian behaviour and witness.

6 Freedom and holiness

1 Corinthians 6

Paul continues to address moral issues. Christians must not grasp at what is not theirs. For example, those with financial or social clout should not use it in the courts to gain personal advantage (perhaps by bribing the judges, as was common practice in civil law cases). Some believers are making grandiose claims about sitting on thrones and sharing in Christ's judgement at the end of time (v. 2; see 4:8; Matthew 19:28). How, then, can they sink to petty acts of manipulation and injustice in daily life?

A grasping attitude can be equally destructive in other areas of life. Paul lists other sins, such as idolatry, drunkenness, verbal abuse and various sexual sins (for detailed discussion of the references to homosexual relationships, see Anthony Thiselton's larger commentary on 1 Corinthians, published 2000). How can Paul say that such 'wrongdoers will not inherit the kingdom of God' (v. 9)? His gospel message offers God's forgiveness of sin (see 1:30; Romans 3:21–26), but, when these sins become habits and patterns of life rather than simply isolated actions, they prevent relationship with God. A lack of resolve to change such behaviour casts doubt on the genuineness of someone's professed commitment to Christ.

The Corinthians love to proclaim their newfound freedom in Christ, as in their slogan 'Liberty to do all things', which Paul quotes (v. 12). Verse 13 begins with what may be another of their favourite catch-phrases, 'Food for the stomach and the stomach for food, but God will do away with the one and the other'. (We cannot easily identify quotations, as ancient Greek did not use quotation marks, so this is a matter of judgement for translators.) This slogan suggests that physical things will pass away, leaving only the immortal soul—which can provide a convenient excuse to do whatever we like with our bodies. On the contrary, Paul argues, the Christian life is not simply a private, inner matter; it is lived out in our bodies (v. 13), which must be holy because the Holy Spirit lives in them (v. 19). Freedom does not mean licence to live exactly how we please, gratifying our selfish desires. Christians are 'bought with a price' (v. 20), so they belong to a new master who has paid for them by his own, costly death.

Guidelines

Here are some questions. Choose those that are most relevant to your situation at present, and reflect on them in the light of what we have read this week.

- Which do you find easier, encouraging or confronting? Can you see the need for both, in your own discipleship and in the building up of the church today?
- What is your attitude towards the Christian leaders you know (including yourself, if you are one)? Think about what good leadership involves. How can we respect and admire good leaders while resisting the urge to create, adore and criticise celebrities, which is in the cultural air that we breathe?

- How central is the cross for you and for your church? Is it tempting to play down this part of the gospel message in today's world?
- Is something threatening or disrupting the unity of your church at present? If so, see if anything in this week's readings is relevant to that situation.
- We live in an information-saturated culture, but what is the difference between information and wisdom? How can we explore the depths of God's wisdom? In what ways does God's wisdom contradict worldly wisdom?
- Many people around us are interested in 'spirituality'. How can we help them to develop their spiritual hunger and find truly nourishing ways to satisfy it?
- We celebrate our freedom in Christ while also hearing God's call to holiness. Does this create any tension in your life at present?

1 Singleness and marriage

1 Corinthians 7:1–16

Having forcefully voiced his own concerns about what is going on in Corinth, Paul now turns to the matters raised by the church in their letter to him (v. 1). Here he shows pastoral sensitivity and flexibility, weighing arguments and acknowledging the complexities of certain issues.

Some in Corinth are saying that 'it is good for a man not to be physically intimate with a woman' (scholars are convinced that Paul is quoting the Corinthians' words in 7:1, not giving his own view). Disdain for anything to do with the human body has led them to insist that truly spiritual people should avoid sex, even between husband and wife. Paul totally rejects this view, insisting that sex is a good and important part of marriage. He sees husband and wife as each giving to the other in sexual intimacy (vv. 2–6); sex is not about asserting power over someone. The ancient world generally saw sex as either a duty (to produce children) or a pleasure that women provided for men. Women were the inferior partner in marriage, with little power compared to the husband's. Paul's picture of husband and wife enjoying mutual intimacy and agreeing on sexual matters in a reciprocal way is a unique view, far ahead of its time.

Paul himself was either single or widowed (v. 8; he had been a leading Pharisee, which usually involved being married). He honours singleness equally alongside marriage: neither state is superior to the other; each can be seen as a gift and calling from God. For some people, singleness can provide liberation from the distractions of family life, freeing them to focus on gospel commitments. For others, however, sexual desire for another person can become so strong that it distracts from gospel priorities more than the commitments of marriage would (vv. 8–9; see also vv. 32–35). In Paul's world, young girls were pressured to marry, and widows to remarry; he urges Christians to resist such unhelpful pressures. In a society where divorce was rife and easy (for men), Paul encourages greater commitment, preserving marriage wherever possible (vv. 10, 11b–13), but he recognises that, in some circumstances, reconciling a couple may prove impossible (vv. 11a, 15). As he considers various scenarios throughout this chapter, Paul shows pastoral sensitivity, not laying down the law but recognising that different circumstances need different responses (vv. 25, 35, 40).

2 My rights and responsibilities

1 Corinthians 8

Food bought in the market at Corinth, particularly meat, often came from the temples, where it had been offered or dedicated to pagan gods such as Zeus or Aphrodite in religious rituals. Sometimes it was actually eaten in the temple precincts, at dinner parties (which might include a courtesy 'nod' towards the idol of the temple, who supposedly presided over the meal). Wealthier Christians would at times be invited to these meals by their non-Christian friends or business contacts. Some Christians in Corinth felt uneasy about eating such food, particularly at these kinds of dinner parties, wondering if it was tainted by idolatry. Memories of their former life, worshipping idols, may still have been fresh in their minds, along with fears of getting sucked back into their old lifestyle. For them, becoming a Christian meant a clean break with the past, a totally new lifestyle—even if that meant severing links with former business contacts, status and lifestyle. Other Christians, by contrast, argued that idols were empty 'nothings', since there was really only one true God (vv. 4–6); therefore any food could be eaten without such scruples. As far as these believers were concerned, it was not tainted or corrupting, and how could they win others to Christ without this social contact?

This confident group claims to know better, to 'possess knowledge'. Paul agrees with some of their views, but their attitude tends to inflate their sense of self-importance rather than building up the church: it takes love to 'build up' (8:1). True knowledge, Paul argues, is not something we achieve or possess by mastering a lot of information; it is an ongoing process of 'coming to know' (v. 2), so Paul challenges those who claim to have knowledge to be aware of the struggles of their insecure brothers and sisters, whom they refer to in a rather superior way as 'the weak'. Is it right to damage their faith and conscience (or 'self-awareness', v. 7) by exercising the freedom to choose? 'No way,' Paul answers: behaving like that is unthinkable (v. 13).

Food from the temples may not be our concern today, but sometimes we see a particular issue one way, convinced that we have understood it, and then have to acknowledge that others see it quite differently because of their different perspective and past experiences.

3 Practise what you preach

1 Corinthians 9:1–18

Words are cheap; costly actions speak louder. Having just asked some in Corinth to forgo their freedom out of love for others, even in ways that might damage their trade and financial interests (ch. 8), Paul feels a need to show that he practises what he preaches. He gives an example from personal experience, not to boast about himself but to show his credibility in asking for sacrifices from others.

As a recognised 'apostle' (a messenger, sent to witness to Christ), Paul could expect hospitality and financial support from those to whom he ministered. This was standard practice in the early churches; for those who were married, such as Peter (Cephas), it included support for their wives who travelled with them (vv. 3–7). Paul acknowledges the validity of this practice (vv. 8–12), but he reminds the believers that when he was in Corinth he chose not to demand this right, preferring to earn his keep from his trade as a tentmaker (Acts 18:3). Why did he willingly choose to forgo his entitlement? Partly out of thankfulness: he was so overwhelmed by the generosity of God's free grace that he wanted, or even felt compelled, to give grace freely to others, by proclaiming the gospel free of charge (vv. 15–18). The joy of doing this felt like reward enough. Paul's passion for sharing the gospel, whatever it might cost, shines through in the section of the letter that follows (9:19–27).

Paul's other reason for refusing payment relates to the culture of the Greco-Roman world: when people gave favours, they expected loyalty in return. If Paul accepted financial support in Corinth, it would come from the wealthier members of the church—those whom Paul is challenging here about their attitudes to 'the weak'. They would become Paul's patrons, expecting him to feel obliged to favour them in return in his preaching and ministry. Paul is determined to give pastoral support to everyone in the church, sometimes giving special attention to the most vulnerable (see 12:22–24), so he declines offers of support, even at the risk of causing offence.

Challenging people to take their responsibilities seriously, rather than always to assert their rights, is not easy in today's world. The message will carry conviction if we back it up in our own actions and lifestyle.

4 Freed to serve the needs of others

1 Corinthians 10:14—11:1

The dangers of idolatry need to be faced. Having reminded his audience of an example from their scriptures (10:1–13), Paul urges them to 'flee from idolatry' (v. 14). Every time they share bread and wine together in the Lord's Supper, they bless 'the cup of blessing'(v. 16)—the Passover cup, which reminds them how God saved his people from slavery in Egypt. This is the exodus story of which all Christ's followers, including the Gentile Corinthians, are now a part. They also share together in the meal as Christ's body, not only remembering his death but also renewing the covenant commitment between Christ and his people (vv. 16–18), so they are not free to pledge loyalty to any other gods.

Paul agrees that idols are ultimately empty and powerless, yet he sees destructive spiritual forces at work in idolatrous worship (vv. 20–21). Paul rarely speaks in these terms. Only here does he refer to 'demons'; elsewhere he talks occasionally of 'powers' and 'spiritual forces of evil' (Romans 8:38; Ephesians 6:12). This largely impersonal language seems to suggest pockets of shadowy power where evil forces are focused, but Paul does not elaborate. His positive concern, however, is clear: anything that damages Christian life and faith is to be avoided.

Rounding off his argument, Paul revisits the favourite Corinthian slogan about freedom (v. 23). It needs to be qualified: Christians must use their freedom in Christ constructively, to build up the church, not to serve their own desires. Rather than 'What do I want?', the key question is always 'Will this be helpful to others?' Love for the other is central in Paul's gospel, as it was in the teaching of Jesus. Once that is established, there is no need to be too fussy in matters such as eating and drinking. Christians can eat and drink as they choose, but if it is likely to cause unhelpful offence (to the host or to a fellow Christian), it is wiser to refrain (vv. 27–30). Glorifying God in all one's actions should always be the priority (v. 31).

Becoming and living like Christ is the central aim for every Christian. Modelling Christ-likeness with integrity, so that others can glimpse what it looks like in practice, is the challenge for every Christian, not least for leaders in the church (11:1).

5 Men and women in worship

1 Corinthians 11:1–16

Women in the Corinthian church have been enjoying newfound freedoms. They sometimes lead others in prayer, and some bring prophetic messages (a type of preaching). Paul approves of women exercising these ministries just as much as men (vv. 4–5).

As so often in Corinth, however, some people are going too far in asserting their freedom, in this case over how they dress. In Roman society, a married woman was expected to wear a hood (or perhaps veil) in public, marking her out as deserving respect; without this, she could be regarded as giving signals of being sexually available. On the other hand, a man who covered his head during worship might look like someone taking part in the worship of Roman gods, and a woman with long, freely flowing hair might resemble those involved in other kinds of pagan worship.

Some Christians in this Roman colony of Corinth, both men and women, may have been trying to throw off restraints and stereotypes, exercising their freedom in Christ by dressing in unconventional ways. Paul warns against this, fearing that it will cause confusion and distract others from focusing on God during worship. Calling the bluff of those who claim to be 'liberated' in this way, he suggests taking the practice to ridiculous extremes (v. 6). If you really want to reject convention, he says, why not appear in public with a shaved head, so that you will look like a boy—or like a prostitute? Paul also describes the hood that a woman wears as a symbol of authority (v. 10), perhaps referring to the authority now given to her to speak out in public worship.

Paul sees differences between the sexes beyond the merely physical ones (vv. 3, 7–12). These differences are not just socially constructed but arise from the way God created humankind. God intends relationships between men and women to be mutual and reciprocal (v. 11). We discover our self-identity in relation to each other and to God, in whose image we are made. Gender difference should prompt mutual respect, not competitiveness or attempts to manipulate one another.

Various details of this passage puzzle commentators, but its big ideas are rich and challenging. Paul celebrates gender differences and affirms roles for women in public worship that were countercultural. In less crucial matters, though, such as dress codes, he affirms accepted cultural practice, in order to prevent people from being distracted when worshipping God.

6 Divisive hospitality

1 Corinthians 11:17–34

Making your home available to others can be a real blessing to the church, but hospitality needs to be combined with gospel attitudes or it can do more harm than good.

Christians in Corinth needed places in which to meet, and these were provided by the wealthier church members, who had larger homes. Sometimes the meetings would involve a communal meal, part of which included an act of worship—'the Lord's Supper', also known today as 'the Eucharist', from the Greek for 'gave thanks' (v. 24), or 'Communion', from another word that Paul uses, meaning 'sharing' (10:16). Those hosting the gatherings seem to have followed the social conventions of the day for dinner parties. Honoured guests would thus be welcomed into the main dining room, while the others gathered in less comfort in an adjoining room (perhaps receiving food and drink of a lesser quality). This was normal, polite etiquette in that society—and Paul rejects it totally for worship gatherings.

In Christ's church, Paul insists, these kinds of social divisions have no place. Those who say that such divisive behaviour is unavoidable in the real world (Paul is probably quoting ironically the views of some of the wealthy Corinthians in verse 19, rather than giving his own view) are just making excuses for bad behaviour. If the result is that some consume too much while others go hungry and are made to feel 'second class', this is outrageous and simply unacceptable (vv. 21–22). The wealthier Christians need greater discernment about what it means to be part of 'the body' of Christ, the church, in solidarity and unity with one another (v. 29). If they complain of getting hungry while waiting for latecomers (perhaps those who had to work late), let them have a snack before coming to the meeting (vv. 33–34)!

Paul turns from criticism to treasured memory—the tradition passed on to him by others, going right back to Jesus himself (vv. 23–26). Like the Passover, this meal revisits and celebrates God's decisive act in saving his people and giving them new life, creating a relationship of covenant commitment between God and people. For Christians, the new Passover centres on the costly self-sacrifice of Christ. When they share this meal, Christians proclaim these truths and witness to being personally part of the story.

Guidelines

What makes a Christian response (a response in accord with Paul's own gospel) to reading what Paul has written? Is it to do what Paul says or to do what Paul does? If we merely do what he says, we read his teaching on behaviour in public worship and hold that it is necessary for women to wear a hat to church (whatever the culture of hats and bare heads around us). If we do what he does, we apply the principles of his theology to our situation as he did to his, and judge for ourselves what will build up the community, exercise God-given authority and gifts, and give no unnecessary offence to those within or without.
R. Evans, *Judge for Yourselves: Reading 1 Corinthians* (DLT, 2003), p. 141

Try 'judging for yourselves', as Paul urges his hearers to do (10:15; 11:13), in your local situation. Consider some of the issues arising from this week's readings.

- Do you, and others in your church, express positive attitudes to sex, marriage and singleness?
- How can you best support those who may be feeling insecure or not confident in their faith?
- Are you willing and able to let go of what you feel entitled to, in order to build up others spiritually?
- How do men and women lead worship in your church? Are you making the best of God-given diversity? Is anything done that proves unhelpfully distracting?
- Are any individuals or groups made to feel second class in the church? If so, are people aware of this?
- How can you exercise hospitality in ways that build up the whole church?

In all these matters, do what Paul encourages his listeners to do: reflect prayerfully on scripture and your own experience, looking for principles and applying them to your situation.

1 Diverse, yet still united

1 Corinthians 12

As we have already seen, some Christians in Corinth claim to be 'spiritual'—but other people make similar claims while worshipping idols. Some use the name of their gods to curse rivals or competitors, a practice that Christians should reject. Verse 3 may be translated simply 'Jesus curse', suggesting that Christians were tempted to try similar manipulative magic (although other interpretations of this puzzling verse are also possible). Christian spirituality must be directed by God the Holy Spirit, not by human desire or self-interest.

Paul directs his hearers away from the term 'spiritual' (*pneumatikon*, v. 1), with its mixed connotations, preferring instead 'spiritual gifts' (*charismata*, vv. 9, 31). These gifts are freely given without charge or favouritism, so they cannot be a sign of status or a cause of pride, distorting the life of the church. The Corinthians' tendency towards disorder and disunity is reflected when they gather for worship, as we saw in the previous chapter; this remains Paul's central concern in chapters 12—14 as he teaches about spiritual gifts.

Paul gives examples of different kinds of 'gifts', 'ministries' and 'activities' in 12:4–11 and 27–31, where he rounds off his argument. They are varied, ranging from healing and prophecy to 'workings of powers' (v. 10), which may include the miraculous, and 'forms of assistance' (v. 28), suggesting administrative help. This list is not conclusive; other gifts and ministries are mentioned elsewhere (see, for example, Romans 12:3–8; Ephesians 4:11–12). No one person is given all these gifts; nor is one particular gift given to each individual: the questions Paul asks in verse 29 are all framed to demand the answer 'no'. Above all, these gifts of the Holy Spirit are given for the common good, to build up the whole church (v. 7).

Diversity is not the enemy of unity. The metaphor of different people working together as a harmonious 'body' was familiar in ancient times. When Plato and Plutarch used the image to encourage solidarity, they directed it at the workers and slaves, urging them to support the governing classes for the sake of unity. Paul reverses this appeal, urging the more respectable to preserve unity by giving special support to those who seem to them weak or less honourable (vv. 20–23; see 8:1–13). The church is called to be a community that turns some of the world's familiar thinking upside-down.

2 Self-giving love

1 Corinthians 13

Many of us have heard this sublime and moving chapter read at weddings. It seems to stand out from its context, with no mention of Christ or the Holy Spirit, like a self-contained poem or hymn.

Yet this chapter turns out to be closely connected to the rest of the letter. It depicts the love that needs to characterise the life of the church, not least its worship, which is the theme of chapters 11—14. This is the 'more excellent way' (12:31), which needs to be the core value of those who 'strive for spiritual gifts' (14:1). Previously Paul warned against knowledge that 'inflates' pride, urging instead love that builds up (4:6; 8:1); now he fills out the picture of that love which 'is not inflated with its own importance' (v. 4). This love 'does not burn with envy'—a pointed contrast to the jealousy and status-seeking that was so damaging in the Corinthian church (see 3:3; 11:18).

In our day, the word 'love' abounds in popular songs, often focused on the needs and longings of the singer; the meaning of the word has become slanted in the direction of self-fulfilment. Paul takes the word *agape*, used in his day for various kinds of love (for example, in the Greek translation of the Old Testament), and invests it with a deeper, richer meaning. This love does not seek fulfilment and security for the self; it decentres the self, seeking what is good for the other. Nor is it manipulative, keeping a record of wrongs, nursing and parading its hurts (vv. 4–7). It is tenacious and will last, in a way that the spiritual gifts most prized by certain rather infantile members of the Corinthian church will not (vv. 8–12; see 14:20). Without this kind of love, all our spiritual talk is simply loud noise. Even the greatest self-sacrifice counts for nothing without love (vv. 1–3).

An instructive exercise for meditation and prayer is to read verses 4–7, inserting the name 'Jesus' wherever Paul has written 'love': glimpses of Christ's character abound. More challenging is to repeat the exercise but this time inserting one's own name instead of 'love'—a sobering reminder that I, like many in Corinth, still have a long way to go on the path of growing in Christ-likeness.

3 Worship that builds up

1 Corinthians 14:1–12, 26–40

The love portrayed in the previous chapter is to permeate all aspects of life, including the use of spiritual gifts in worship (v. 1). This will lead to a desire to do what is good for others rather than simply oneself, showing self-restraint when necessary for the sake of the church as a whole.

The gift of tongues mentioned here is a form of personal prayer, perhaps in an unknown language or perhaps simply an inarticulate expression of praise or longing addressed to God from the depths of the self (v. 2; see Romans 8:26). Paul affirms the value of this spiritual gift for the individual who is given it, but he sees more value for the church in the gift of prophecy (vv. 4–5). Those who prophesy bring some form of God-given message (which may include both pastoral and evangelistic preaching: see 14:24–25). This builds up the church as a whole—the key priority that Paul keeps emphasising (vv. 12, 26). Speaking in tongues builds up the individual but not the church (unless the speaker, or someone else present, can explain what they are saying so that it makes sense to everyone: vv. 13–17).

Worship in Corinth was clearly lively and active, with all kinds of people involved. Some of our churches need to learn from that! Paul wants to encourage much that is going on, and, to enable this, he suggests some practical 'house rules' (vv. 26–33). These are not intended to quench the life and spontaneity but to protect it from being manipulated by self-indulgent individuals and descending into chaos.

What does Paul mean by 'Women should be silent' (v. 34)? A little earlier he was affirming the role of women as leaders in public prayer and prophecy (11:4–5). Is he now contradicting himself? Some commentators see 14:33b–36 as a later addition, not written by Paul, since it disrupts the flow of the passage, interrupting the argument about prophets. If Paul did write these verses, he may have been commenting on a particular problem in Corinth. When someone shared a prophetic message in worship, those listening were encouraged to 'test' or 'sift' what was said (v. 29); perhaps a few women were misusing this freedom to interrogate or undermine certain speakers, particularly their own husbands. Using public worship to continue domestic disputes in this way would have been very destructive (v. 35).

4 A message of death and life

1 Corinthians 15:1–22

What message did the earliest Christian evangelists and preachers proclaim? We find a few summaries and soundbites in the book of Acts. Today's passage gives us a glimpse of what Paul preached—'the gospel that I proclaimed to you' (v. 1). What the Corinthians received from him, he in turn had received and handed on—a tradition to be guarded and preserved. Here is a creed of essential facts to be known, but also one on which believers 'take their stand', something they commit themselves to and build their lives upon.

Paul's creed and message were centred on Jesus' death and resurrection. Christ died 'for' our sins: his death put right the problem caused by human sins. Mention of his burial emphasises that he really did die: he was not some heavenly phantom or a human who simply fainted on the cross and woke up later in the tomb. Christ 'was raised' by the power of his Father working through the Holy Spirit. All this was 'according to the scriptures'—the ultimate expression of the character and promises of God found in the Old Testament, expressed now in the faithful Servant-Son of God.

All these events were witnessed by various people, ranging from Jesus' closest disciples to a crowd of more than 500 people, some of whom are still alive when Paul is writing (so their testimony can be verified by anyone who wants to ask them about it). Last among the witnesses, Paul names himself, having met the risen Christ on the road to Damascus

(Acts 9:5). Paul emphasises God's miraculous grace in giving him new life, describing himself as 'untimely born' or 'an aborted foetus' (v. 8)—perhaps an insulting expression that others threw at him.

Paul stresses the reality of Christ's resurrection because some in Corinth are denying it (v. 12). Perhaps some reject any possibility of resurrection, or say that it could happen 'spiritually' but not literally to a human body. Others may be saying that Christians are already raised from the dead, with no further resurrection event to hope for. Paul rejects such views as pitiful (v. 19). He insists that human bodies really can be raised: Christ's was, giving a paradigm for what we can look forward to (v. 20 onwards). Here is gospel-based hope, which he explores in the verses that follow.

5 Renewed bodies

1 Corinthians 15:29–58

Having begun his letter by pointing to the cross of Christ and its implications (1:10—2:5), Paul ends it by expounding Christ's resurrection. Belief and hope in the resurrection can transform lives. The puzzling reference to 'baptism for the sake of the dead' (15:29) may be an example of this, if it refers to those who become Christians and seek baptism for a particular reason—because the confident hope of eternal life that they saw in a dying Christian friend inspired and convinced them.

Paul insists that Christians will be raised in physical bodies. He chides any who find this idea impossible to imagine, giving analogies from the created world (vv. 36–38). Seeds, for example, end their existence by being transformed into something else, a plant, which has continuity with the seed from which it grew. The seed decays when it is sown, then is transformed into exactly the opposite—a thriving plant, full of life and vitality. Similarly, our earthly bodies decay and die but will be transformed into a 'spiritual body' (v. 44), by which Paul means not a nonphysical body but a physical body perfectly energised and transformed by the Holy Spirit. The new body will be glorious, perhaps like Jesus' body when he was transfigured (Mark 9:2–3). Ordinary 'flesh and blood' people, full of weakness and sinfulness, need to be transformed into something different, something holy, before they can enter this glorious life and be able to meet God face to face (v. 50).

This transformation will happen 'in the blinking of an eye' (v. 52), when Christ returns as judge and ushers in a renewed creation (see Romans 8:18–25). For Christians, dying is simply like falling asleep; we will awake suddenly, like an army woken by the morning trumpet call, to join those who are still living when Christ returns. The deadliness of death—like the fatal sting of a snake's fangs or a scorpion's tail—is disarmed by the victory of Christ in his death and resurrection, so death has lost its horror for those who are in Christ.

Until that day comes, its anticipation motivates us for Christian service (v. 58). God's victory and grace, and the hope of transforming glory to come, prompt our gratitude and inspire us to offer all that we are for 'the work of the Lord'.

6 In this together

1 Corinthians 16

In the opening words of this letter, Paul reminded the Corinthians that they were part of the worldwide church (1:2). In this closing chapter, he revisits that truth and fleshes it out with practical examples. An excessive focus on our own local context can be a weakness, particularly if it is combined with pride and independence. There is so much for us to learn from others in the wider church and so much for us to contribute to their needs and spiritual growth. Awareness of 'the other' and mutual solidarity with them have been themes throughout the letter. That solidarity needs to extend beyond our own church and locality.

Part of the challenge and privilege of being the body of Christ comes in financial solidarity. Paul urges the Corinthians to take part in the collection that he has been organising in other churches in the region (vv. 1–4). The fact that the money collected will go to the church in Jerusalem adds a further dimension: Paul is asking Gentile Christians to show solidarity with their Jewish brothers and sisters. Crossing cultural and ethnic boundaries in this way could be a challenge for all concerned.

Paul's instructions on giving are thoroughly practical. Giving should be a regular weekly discipline, done freely and thoughtfully. Christians should give out of their abundance and with regard to others' need. The money should be handled with transparency, by a group of people trusted by the givers.

Paul is an evangelist and pastor but not a lone, freelance individual. His ministry involves various co-workers and supporting churches; we glimpse some of them in verses 5–20. Strategic planning for the welfare of them all is important to him. At present, despite the problems in Corinth, his priority is to remain in Ephesus, because of the window of opportunity open to him there. Apollos is unwilling to travel to Corinth just yet (perhaps because of the way some Corinthian admirers are misusing his name, seeking to drive a wedge between him and his co-worker, Paul: see 1:12; 3:4). As a compromise, Paul sends Timothy to represent him and challenges the Corinthians not to look down on this young colleague.

Paul closes with warm greetings from Christians with him in Ephesus, as well as reminders of a central concern—the importance of love (vv. 14, 22, 24). His last word is a declaration of his own love for the Corinthians.

Guidelines

Which aspects of this week's readings have struck a chord with you? Think about how they speak into your own spiritual life, and the life of your church.

- Do you know what your spiritual gifts are? You probably have a number of them. Others in the church may help you identify them. Look for ways to use your gifts and to encourage the development of other people's gifts.
- Does something hold you back from self-giving love? It could be apathy or selfish pride, or it could be hurts from past experiences that make you wary of trusting others. If this area is a challenge for you, pray about it, perhaps with a friend.
- Does your worship on Sundays or at midweek meetings get people involved and enthused, without becoming chaotic? Think of ways in which you can nourish and strengthen each other more in worship, particularly through the words that are spoken.

- What is your hope for the future, in this life and beyond it? Take some time to reflect on Jesus' cross and resurrection and our own dying and rising. How does your hope affect the way you want to live here and now, in this physical, embodied life?
- Does your regular financial giving need reviewing? You might want to think about how you plan it, and ways in which it can benefit the wider body of Christ.
- What should be the priorities for you and your church in this next phase of life?

If we want one sentence to sum up the whole of 1 Corinthians, it might be 'Knowledge puffs up, but love builds up' (8:1). Reflect on the meaning of these words for Paul and the Corinthian church. Pray about their meaning for your own spiritual growth, family and work relationships, and particularly the life of your church.

FURTHER READING

R. Evans, *Judge for Yourselves: Reading 1 Corinthians*, DLT, 2003. Concise and clear. Arranges the letter in themes, linked with some of Paul's other letters.

M.R. Malcolm, *The World of 1 Corinthians*, Authentic, 2012. Explores the Greco-Roman culture of the letter through pictures and ancient literature.

A.C. Thiselton, *1 Corinthians: A shorter exegetical and pastoral commentary*, Eerdmans, 2006. An outstanding applied commentary by a leading scholar, which I have drawn on a lot in these notes.

N.T. Wright, *Paul for Everyone: 1 Corinthians*, SPCK, 2003. Succinct scholarship expressed in a refreshing style.

Supporting
The Gift of Years
with a gift in your will

For many charities, income from legacies is crucial in enabling them to plan ahead, and often provides the funding to develop new projects. A legacy to support BRF's ministry would make a huge difference.

As we're living longer, BRF's The Gift of Years (www.thegiftofyears.org.uk) celebrates the blessings of long life—but it doesn't underestimate the difficulties. As more and more churches seek to respond to the challenges of an ageing population, The Gift of Years signposts practical ways in which our later years can be infinitely more fulfilling, intense and rewarding.

The vision and purpose of The Gift of Years is:

- to resource the spiritual journey of older people.
- to resource ministry among older people, wherever they may be—in congregations, in care homes or in their own homes.
- to emphasise the opportunities that greater longevity brings, so that our later years might be some of the most spiritually fertile years of our earthly life.
- to encourage and enable younger generations to consider what constitutes 'successful ageing' and so prepare for more positive experiences in older age.
- to 'join up the dots' to make more widely known the wealth of resources and courses already available and the organisations and individuals working in this field.

Throughout its history, BRF's ministry has been enabled thanks to the generosity of those who have shared its vision and supported its work, both by giving during their lifetime and also through legacy gifts.

A legacy gift would help fund the development and sustainability of BRF's The Gift of Years into the future. We hope you may consider a legacy gift to help us continue to take this work forward.

For further information about making a gift to BRF in your will or to discuss how a specific bequest could be used to develop our ministry, please contact Sophie Aldred (Head of Fundraising) or Richard Fisher (Chief Executive) by email at fundraising@brf.org.uk or by phone on 01865 319700.

The BRF

Magazine

Celebrating 20 years of Barnabas for Children

Olivia Warburton

When BRF's Barnabas Children's Ministry is mentioned, what comes to mind for you? Is it our successful schools programme of Barnabas RE Days and INSET, our Barnabas in Churches website teeming with creative ideas, or our range of published resources, developed over the past 20 years?

In 1995, four years after BRF made the decision to start producing books as well as Bible reading notes, the Barnabas imprint was launched. Over the years, highlights have included titles as varied as Jenny Hyson's *The Easter Garden: Following in the Footsteps of Jesus*, Margaret Withers' *Welcome to the Lord's Table* course book for Communion preparation, the primary school resources *Stories for Interactive Assemblies* and *Stories of Everyday Saints*, and our edition of Anno Domini's *My First Bible*.

Barnabas began with a focus on publishing books for children under eleven, and our range of colour gift books continues to grow, with picture story books, sticker books and children's Bibles. Look out for the lavishly illustrated *Barnabas 365 Story Bible*, available from this February.

It then became apparent that there was a need to equip those working with children, both in churches and schools. On the schools side,

we now produce classroom material for RE teachers and Collective Worship resources that also have strong take-up by church visitors leading assemblies in schools. Our new publication *RE in the Classroom with 4–5s*, by Helen Jaeger, offers biblically based lesson plans for use with an age group for whom there is currently a shortage of appropriate RE teaching material.

We also produce a wide range of material for churches, increasingly with an eye to an all-age context alongside more traditional children's groups. *Creative Ideas for Lent and Easter* by Jane

Tibbs provides a wealth of seasonal activities for different ages and interests, and coming soon is *50 Praise, Pray and Play Sessions* by Rona Orme, providing easy-to-run all-age outlines for use throughout the week with families in the community. We are also respected providers of training resources for children's workers, as well as curriculum material for key moments in the spiritual journey such as baptism and confirmation.

Another key area of activity within Barnabas for Children is in encouraging and supporting faith in the home. Our new title *Exploring God's Love in Everyday Life* by Yvonne Morris, a follow-up to *Side by Side with God in Everyday Life*, offers 20 readings, reflections and prayers based on 1 Corinthians 13 for parents and children to share together.

On a larger scale, our new *Barnabas Family Bible*, developed in partnership with Bible Society, takes families right the way through the Bible story, helping them to share a reflective and interactive time together through Bible story extracts, comments, questions, prayer and activity ideas, visual aids, key verses and Old and New Testament story links. James Catford, Group Chief Executive of Bible Society, writes:

Bible Society believes that every child has the right to experience the Bible for themselves and that's why we're excited to be partnering with BRF in the publication of The Barnabas Family Bible. *This book encourages families to sit and explore the riches of the Bible together, reading the Bible text of 110 popular stories while delving deeper through activities, questions and prayers. Millions of people around the world have grown up with the Bible stories. It is our hope that* The Barnabas Family Bible *will enable families to keep the Bible alive for another generation.*

Children's and family ministry is changing fast, and, as we continue to respond to the needs across our churches and in our homes, there is much that is both exciting and challenging as we look ahead. Our hope is that we can indeed help children and adults alike to keep the Bible alive for another generation… and beyond!

Olivia Warburton is Commissioning Editor for Barnabas books for Children and Families, and author of Teaching Narnia: A cross-curricular classroom and assembly resource for RE teachers *(Barnabas in Schools, 2013).*

Guidelines 30th anniversary

David Spriggs

'Where's the birthday cake?' Yesterday I was at my grandson's party! Yes, excitement, presents and people young and old may be important to commemorate a birthday when you are seven instead of six, but the cake is essential. Of course, parents and grandparents are not only sharing the excitement but are also grateful for the privilege of seeing a young life unfold.

Unfortunately I can't offer you any birthday cake but I am pleased that I can invite you to our celebration. In this issue we are celebrating not seven but 30 years of *Guidelines*, and we can all be both excited and grateful. We're excited that, in spite of all the pressures on publishing, reading and especially Bible reading, BRF had the foresight and courage to start this new venture in 1985 and it is still going strong. We know from emails and letters, as well as the number of copies published, that *Guidelines* meets a real need and benefits people in many areas of Christian life today. We are therefore grateful to God for calling BRF into this venture and for linking people with this resource. We invite you to share this sense of gratitude with us.

To help us all, let's consider more precisely what we are celebrating. After all, there are many notes available from BRF and other providers—but *Guidelines* offers something unique in the regular Bible reading notes marketplace. Its primary intention is to 'enable all its readers to interpret and apply the biblical text with confidence in today's world, while helping to equip church leaders as they meet the challenge of mission and disciple-building'.

At the heart of *Guidelines* is not the notes but the Bible. Over a four- to five-year period we aim to cover most of the New Testament, and the Old Testament in seven to eight years. Stimulating people to engage with the scriptures is our vital task, but it is not *our* selection, and not the 'comfortable' words alone. We recognise that all of scripture is God's gift to his people, not just the easier sections.

Before we can 'interpret and apply' the Bible, we need to engage with it appropriately. This appropriate 'deeper' engagement is what *Guidelines* exists for, and, to facilitate it, we seek out the best biblical scholars to illuminate the text with both their knowledge and their profound faith. Many of the contributions come from people who are working on major new commentaries. I am constantly surprised that these very busy scholars are prepared to accept the challenge of condensing their own work into manageable 'chunks' for us. There are very few who refuse an invitation to write for us, and that is because of the excellent reputation that Guidelines has earned during 30 thirty years. In no small measure, this is due to the hard work and inspiration of its different editors and contributors over that time.

We recognise, too, that scripture is the core text of all the churches. We seek to reflect this by including writers whose spiritual homes are in all the main traditions, especially the Anglican one but also the Roman Catholic, the Free Churches and the newer emerging streams. Most of our writers are thoroughly immersed in the challenges of living out our faith today and the worship and mission of these churches. Many of them work in higher level theological education, but we also include people whose main focus is their local church or diocesan work. Interpreting the Bible involves praxis as well as study, and such writers have a particularly valuable contribution to make by providing notes that focus on mission, leadership and discipleship.

Recently a large survey of 400,000 individuals and 1500 churches attempted to discern what drives spiritual growth ('growing in love of God and love of others'). The survey found that there were many factors at different levels of maturation. However, reflection on scripture was the only catalyst that appeared at every level. An article summarising the research for the Centenary of the Edinburgh Conference of 2010 ends with the following challenge:

Spiritually vibrant churches have spiritually vibrant leaders... Do you take time to reflect on Scripture for yourself, apart from preparing to teach, lead a group, or preach a sermon? Are you cultivating a passion for God's Word that is contagious?

N.S. LEWIS, 'LESSONS LEARNED FROM THE REVEAL SPIRITUAL LIFE SURVEY' IN *BIBLE IN MISSION* (REGNUM, 2013), P. 263

Incisive and illuminating insights into the biblical text are at the core of *Guidelines* but, in the end, if the Bible is not transforming us, then it is failing to perform its role. Eugene Peterson, the author of THE MESSAGE, has some deeply challenging things to say to us here: 'There is no word of God that God does not intend to be lived by us... every word of

God revealed and read in the Bible is there to be conceived and born in us' (*Eat This Book*, Hodder and Stoughton, 2006, p. 114). Here again, *Guidelines* seeks to keep the Bible, not the writers' notes or the reader's response, at the heart of this process. There is immense transformative power in the scriptures, properly understood. We hope that the notes, rather than rushing readers to personal introspection, will encourage them to stick to the scriptures, allowing God's word to work on their minds and imaginations, their wills and behaviour.

Of course, this is neither an automatic nor an enforced transformation; rather (again, in the words of Peterson), 'God doesn't make us do any of this: God's word is personal address, inviting, commanding, challenging, rebuking, judging, comforting, directing. But not forcing... We are given space and freedom to answer, to enter into the conversation' (*Eat This Book*, p. 109). So at the end of the week, the concluding 'Guidelines' section offers ways in which this process of transformation, through engagement with the text, can become more deeply rooted within us.

Guidelines, in other words, seeks to treat us as adults who can cope with the whole of scripture, who value the ongoing fruits of scholarship and are serious in working out our faith and life within both our culture and the churches of today. The notes both direct us to the Bible as central and seek to enable us to attend carefully and consistently to that centre. Equally, however, *Guidelines* acknowledges that we need the ongoing attention and renewal that comes to us from God through the Holy Spirit.

The transformative work of scripture is not limited to the individual or even Christian communities. Ultimately, scripture is (in Lesslie Newbigin's words) 'the story of the world', so *Guidelines* helps us to apply scripture to our world—or, perhaps better, helps us to 'see' the world through a transformed imagination and then join with God in his mission.

It is with deep appreciation of the contribution of *Guidelines* in 'unfolding' scripture that I invite you to celebrate its 30th birthday with me, to offer praise to God for all it has achieved and to pray for an increasing and effective role for *Guidelines* in the future.

Your decrees are wonderful... The unfolding of your word gives light. (Psalm 119:129–130, NRSV)

David Spriggs has retired from Bible Society but continues his work with them as a consultant. His main role is as a team minister at the Hinckley Baptist Church, where he has special responsibility to work with the leadership.

Recommended reading

Kevin Ball

One of the biggest headaches for parents of teenagers is convincing them that parents do have a bit of wisdom to pass on that is valuable. But is it just teens who are so difficult to persuade? As human beings, we seem have a 'standard operating procedure' which dictates that we value knowledge only if we have discovered it for ourselves rather than by embracing the hard-won experience of others.

What about issues of faith? Personal discovery is vital for any true, deep relationship with God to grow, but there is also so much that can be learnt from past travellers if we care to look. Prayer is one of the areas in which many people struggle. John Twisleton offers help in his new book *Using the Jesus Prayer*, unwrapping from his personal experience the value of this very ancient prayer, a prayer well known by name but perhaps not so well known in practice as a key step to contemplation.

Fiona Stratta's first book for BRF, *Walking with Gospel Women* (2012), was a bestseller, helping individuals and groups to enter the world of New Testament women through carefully crafted personal monologues that told of each woman's encounter with Jesus. Through her stories, Fiona enabled readers to feel the emotions, concerns and passions of these long-gone individuals—to walk in their shoes and discover that, despite the passing of time, their emotions were very similar to ours today and can offer effective, relevant help for our Christian journey. In her new book, *Walking with Old Testament Women*, Fiona turns her attention to women even further away from us in time but still powerfully able to pass on wisdom in the life-issues that really matter.

Caroline George discovered the wisdom of age by leading a women's fellowship group. She found that, although advanced in years, the women had much to offer, and her times with the group became the catalyst for her new book, *Living Liturgies*, a resource for those leading and pastoring older generations.

Passing on our experience of faith is a key part of Christian witness.

We do that effectively at BRF through the ministry of Messy Church, which is reaching out around the world to unchurched families. Messy Churches need resourcing, and this month we publish two new books full of ideas: the *Messy Family Fun* holiday club programme and *Messy Easter*, which offers three complete Messy sessions for Lent, Holy Week and Easter.

You can keep up to date with all of our new titles and offers by signing up to the regular BRF email at www.brfonline.org.uk/enews-signup/

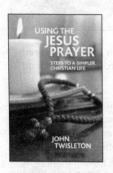

Using the Jesus Prayer
Steps to a simpler Christian life
John Twisleton

pb, 978 1 84101 778 5, 128 pages, £6.99

How can I live a simpler Christian life? Is there a summary of faith that's clear, memorable and portable? An effective, biblically based guide to praying at all times? An aid that can restore inner peace amid the busyness and the noise of daily life, to bring communion with God?

'Yes,' says parish priest John Twisleton. John has used the Jesus Prayer for many years and, in this new book, he shares his experience of its use, so that you may also enjoy its rich treasure.

John begins the book by reflecting on the good news intrinsic to the Jesus Prayer, and goes on to show how the spiritual discipline of repeating the prayer is built upon its base in scripture. He then changes gear to look at how the methods used to combat anxiety and mental distraction in popular Eastern 'mindfulness' exercises can be found in the Jesus Prayer as a 'God-given mantra'. The book concludes with practical advice about saying the Jesus Prayer, how it helps in relating worship to life, and its usefulness in building up the integrity of Christian believers.

Walking with Old Testament Women
More interactive Bible meditations
Fiona Stratta

pb, 978 1 84101 718 1, 176 pages, £7.99

Superficially, women today may seem very different from the women of the Old Testament who lived so long ago, but, as we hear their stories, we discover that we have much in common: joy and heartache, love and jealousy, difficult choices and the need for patience, wisdom and courage. In our wider society, too, there are dysfunctional families beset by difficulties, and many women across the world have little personal choice or freedom.

Fiona Stratta, author of the BRF bestselling book *Walking with Gospel Women*, provides 21 imaginative, Ignatian-style monologues and studies based on the biblical accounts of Old Testament women including Sarah, Ruth, Bathsheba, Hannah and Tamar. Each character tells her own story. Fiona provides points for reflection and discussion after each monologue, enabling issues to be explored and links to New Testament teaching made. Of greatest importance, we see in these narratives God's wonderful grace, his undeserved favour and blessing, touching the lives of these women, and discover that the same grace is available to us. Suitable for both group and individual use.

Living Liturgies
Transition time resources for services, prayer and conversation with older people
Caroline George

pb, 978 0 85746 323 4, 128 pages, £7.99

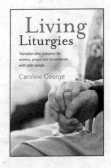

This is a creative and original book of liturgies and reflections for use in worship and pastoral ministry with older people, who are moving from the 'third age' to the more dependent 'fourth age' of life. Developed by the author after many years of working in church and community settings with older people, the book provides an invaluable resource for those embarking on this ministry as well as those wanting inspiration for their ongoing work. The book also includes wider reflections on ageing and spirituality.

Messy Family Fun
A five-day holiday club and one-day fun day for all the family!
Lucy Moore

pb, 978 0 85746 305 0, 96 pages, £9.99

Messy Family Fun provides a holiday club programme for the whole family or for children coming with an adult. It offers five consecutive days of two-hour sessions followed by a meal, reflecting the values of Messy Church (Christ-centred, creativity, celebration, hospitality, all-age), and includes background and principles for this model, alongside session plans, downloadable templates and follow-up ideas. There is also a one-day Messy Church Fun Day outline, which can be used as a trial run for the full holiday club and/or as a community event to attract new families.

Messy Easter
3 complete sessions and a treasure trove of craft ideas for Lent, Easter and Pentecost
Jane Leadbetter

pb, 978 1 84101 717 4, 96 pages, £5.99

Three complete sessions for Lent, Holy Week and Easter, together with a wealth of activities to extend the range of excitingly messy activities for your Messy Church, including creative prayers, games, food crafts and ideas for organising an Easter trail. Craft templates and a session planning grid are provided.

To order copies of any of these books, please turn to the order form on page 155, or visit www.brfonline.org.uk.

An extract from
Reflecting the Glory

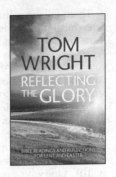

In BRF's Lent book for 2015 (first published in 1998), author Tom Wright draws on New Testament passages to show that through God's Holy Spirit, the suffering but also the glory of Christ can be incarnate in our lives, enabling us to be the people of God for the world. The following extract is a comment on John 13:1–20.

Jesus' 'hour' (v. 1) was the moment when he was going to accomplish the mission for which he had been sent into the world. John characterises this moment in terms of departing from the world and going to the Father, which is why the following chapters are known as the 'farewell discourses'… Still in the first verse of the passage, John says that Jesus had loved his followers 'to the end'. This phrase 'to the end' doesn't just mean that he went on loving them as long as there was breath in his body, although that was true as well. John clearly means that he loved them to the uttermost; there was nothing that love could do for them that he did not do for them. And this introduces us to the next scene, when Jesus enacts, symbolically, the love of God.

John notes that Judas, the son of Simon Iscariot, had already found it in his heart to betray Jesus. As betrayal involved an act of accusation, of accusing Jesus before the chief priests and the Jewish rulers, John attributes this betrayal to the devil, who in Hebrew has the name 'the Satan', which means 'the accuser'. Judas now personified the sense of accusation that had been hanging over Jesus for much of his ministry, and that was about to confront him openly. Verse 3, however, describes Jesus as knowing that the Father had given all things into his hands; he had come from God and was returning to God… He was committed to a course of action which was the very embodiment, or, to use the Latin-based word, the incarnation of the love of God.

After supper, to express that graphically, he got up from the table, took off his outer robe, tied a towel around himself, poured water into a basin and washed the disciples' feet. When John describes that sequence, he is describing not only the action of Jesus at the table but also the action of Jesus in coming down from God, laying aside the garments of glory, taking instead the form of a servant, girding himself with a towel and doing for his friends the work that a servant would normally do…

There follows a little scene of what might almost be called comedy. Peter misunderstands. He does not want Jesus washing his feet. But Jesus insists: 'You don't understand this at the moment,' he says to Peter, 'but you will later.' Peter goes on blustering: 'I'm not going to let you wash my feet.' And Jesus responds, rather sharply: 'If I don't wash you, you can have no part in me, no share in what I'm doing. You must let me wash you.' Peter's innate human pride means he doesn't want to be a humble leader. He might have to be humble in turn, and that would never do. But when he is faced with the threat that, unless he goes through with it, he won't have any part in Jesus' work, then, typically, he flips to the other extreme and says: 'You had better wash all of me—Lord, not my feet only but my hands and my head!' Jesus replies (v. 10), 'One who has bathed does not need to wash, except for the feet, but is entirely clean. And you are clean, though not all of you.' In other words, he has already accepted Peter; he has already cleaned him. But, as Peter walks through the world, his feet will get dirty again and once more need washing. In the same way, when we pray the Lord's Prayer we don't have to start every time as totally unforgiven sinners. We come as God's beloved children, saying 'Our Father in heaven', but halfway through the prayer we admit gladly and freely that we have some things that need sorting out, some problems that need addressing today. And it will be the same tomorrow.

So Jesus washes the disciples' feet, and explains to Peter what it means, how it connects with their sharing in his life, his glory, his work. When he has finished, put on his robe again and returned to the table, he explains further to them the significance of what he has done… Well, he says, you call me Teacher and Lord (v. 13), and you are right to do so, because that is what I am. You must learn, though, that if your Lord and Teacher has washed your feet, you also should wash one another's feet. Jesus is deliberately standing the normal social order on its head, turning the values of the world upside-down…

Throughout all this, Jesus is aware that one of those sitting at the table, one of those whose feet he has washed, is about to get up and leave the company, never to return. The only time they will see him again is when he appears in the garden to betray his master. Jesus is less concerned about that, however, than about conveying to his disciples the meaning of his actions. This is what it means to be equal with God, to reveal the glory of God. Loving his followers to the uttermost, he wants to bequeath them this new way of life which is no less than embodying the love of God—love that was expressed uniquely in Jesus, but then given by his Spirit to all his followers.

To order a copy of this book, please turn to the order form on page 155.

SUPPORTING BRF'S MINISTRY

As a Christian charity, BRF is involved in eight complementary areas.

- **BRF** (www.brf.org.uk) resources adults for their spiritual journey through Bible reading notes, books and Quiet Days. BRF also provides the infrastructure that supports our other specialist ministries.
- **Foundations21** (www.foundations21.net) provides flexible and innovative ways for individuals and groups to explore their Christian faith and discipleship through a multimedia internet-based resource.
- **Messy Church** (www.messychurch.org.uk), led by Lucy Moore, enables churches all over the UK (and increasingly abroad) to reach children and adults beyond the fringes of the church.
- **Barnabas in Churches** (www.barnabasinchurches.org.uk) helps churches to support, resource and develop their children's ministry with the under-11s more effectively .
- **Barnabas in Schools** (www.barnabasinschools.org.uk) enables primary school children and teachers to explore Christianity creatively and bring the Bible alive within RE and Collective Worship.
- **Faith in Homes** (www.faithinhomes.org.uk) supports families to explore and live out the Christian faith at home.
- **Who Let The Dads Out** (www.wholetthedadsout.org) inspires churches to engage with dads and their pre-school children.
- **The Gift of Years** (www.brf.org.uk/thegiftofyears) celebrates the blessings of long life and seeks to meet the spiritual needs of older people.

At the heart of BRF's ministry is a desire to equip adults and children for Christian living—helping them to read and understand the Bible, explore prayer and grow as disciples of Jesus. We need your help to make an impact on the local church, local schools and the wider community.

- You could support BRF's ministry with a one-off gift or regular donation (using the response form on page 153).
- You could consider making a bequest to BRF in your will.
- You could encourage your church to support BRF as part of your church's giving to home mission—perhaps focusing on a specific area of our ministry, or a particular member of our Barnabas team.
- Most important of all, you could support BRF with your prayers.

If you would like to discuss how a specific gift or bequest could be used in the development of our ministry, please phone 01865 319700 or email enquiries@brf.org.uk.

Whatever you can do or give, we thank you for your support.

GUIDELINES SUBSCRIPTIONS

Please note our subscription rates 2015–2016. From the May 2015 issue, the new subscription rates will be:

Individual subscriptions covering 3 issues for under 5 copies, payable in advance (including postage and packing):

	UK	Eur/Economy	Standard
GUIDELINES each set of 3 p.a.	£16.35	£24.00	£27.60
GUIDELINES 3-year sub (i.e. 9 issues)	£42.75	N/A	N/A

Group subscriptions covering 3 issues for 5 copies or more, sent to ONE UK address (post free).

GUIDELINES	£12.90	each set of 3 p.a.

Overseas group subscription rates available on request.
Contact enquiries@brf.org.uk.

Please note that the annual billing period for Group Subscriptions runs from 1 May to 30 April.

Copies of the notes may also be obtained from Christian bookshops:

GUIDELINES	£4.30 each copy

Visit www.biblereadingnotes.org.uk for information about our other Bible reading notes and Apple apps for iPhone and iPod touch.

GL0115

BRF MINISTRY APPEAL RESPONSE FORM

I want to help BRF by funding some of its core ministries. Please use my gift for:

❏ Where most needed ❏ Barnabas Children's Ministry ❏ Foundations21
❏ Messy Church ❏ Who Let The Dads Out? ❏ The Gift of Years

Please complete all relevant sections of this form and print clearly.

Title _____ First name/initials _____ Surname _____

Address _____

_____ Postcode _____

Telephone _____ Email _____

Regular giving

If you would like to give by direct debit, please tick the box below and fill in details:

❏ I would like to make a regular gift of £ _____ per month / quarter / year
(delete as appropriate) by Direct Debit. (Please complete the form on page 159.)

If you would like to give by standing order, please contact Debra McKnight (tel: 01865
319700; email debra.mcknight@brf.org.uk; write to BRF address).

One-off donation

Please accept my special gift of
❏ £10 ❏ £50 ❏ £100 (other) £ _____ by

❏ Cheque / Charity Voucher payable to 'BRF'
❏ Visa / Mastercard / Charity Card
(delete as appropriate)

Name on card _____

Card no. ❏❏❏❏ ❏❏❏❏ ❏❏❏❏ ❏❏❏❏

Start date ❏❏ ❏❏ Expiry date ❏❏ ❏❏

Security code ❏❏❏

Signature _____ Date _____

❏ I would like to give a legacy to BRF. Please send me further information.

❏ I want BRF to claim back tax on this gift.
(If you tick this box, please fill in gift aid declaration overleaf.)

Please detach and send this completed form to: BRF, 15 The Chambers, Vineyard,
Abingdon OX14 3FE. BRF is a Registered Charity (No.233280)

GIFT AID DECLARATION

Bible Reading Fellowship

Please treat as Gift Aid donations all qualifying gifts of money made
today ☐ in the past 4 years ☐ in the future ☐ (tick all that apply)

I confirm I have paid or will pay an amount of Income Tax and/or Capital Gains Tax for each tax year (6 April to 5 April) that is at least equal to the amount of tax that all the charities that I donate to will reclaim on my gifts for that tax year. I understand that other taxes such as VAT or Council Tax do not qualify. I understand the charity will reclaim 25p of tax on every £1 that I give.

☐ My donation does not qualify for Gift Aid.

Signature

Date

Notes:
1. Please notify BRF if you want to cancel this declaration, change your name or home address, or no longer pay sufficient tax on your income and/or capital gains.

2. If you pay Income Tax at the higher/additional rate and want to receive the additional tax relief due to you, you must include all your Gift Aid donations on your Self-Assessment tax return or ask HM Revenue and Customs to adjust your tax code.

BRF PUBLICATIONS ORDER FORM

Please send me the following book(s):	Quantity	Price	Total
713 6 Barnabas Family Bible (M. Payne & J. Butcher)	_____	£9.99	_____
245 9 Creative Ideas for Lent & Easter (J. Tibbs)	_____	£8.99	_____
323 4 Living Liturgies (C. George)	_____	£7.99	_____
717 4 Messy Easter (J. Leadbetter)	_____	£5.99	_____
305 0 Messy Family Fun (L. Moore)	_____	£9.99	_____
3556 0 Reflecting the Glory (T. Wright)	_____	£8.99	_____
138 4 Ten-Minute Easter Activity Book (B. James)	_____	£3.99	_____
778 5 Using the Jesus Prayer (J. Twisleton)	_____	£6.99	_____
010 3 Walking with Gospel Women (F. Stratta)	_____	£7.99	_____
718 1 Walking with Old Testament Women (F. Stratta)	_____	£7.99	_____

Total cost of books £ _____
Donation £ _____
Postage and packing £ _____
TOTAL £ _____

POSTAGE AND PACKING CHARGES				
order value	UK	Europe	Surface	Air Mail
£7.00 & under	£1.25	£3.00	£3.50	£5.50
£7.01–£30.00	£2.25	£5.50	£6.50	£10.00
Over £30.00	free	prices on request		

Please complete the payment details below and send with payment to: **BRF, 15 The Chambers, Vineyard, Abingdon OX14 3FE**

Name _____

Address _____

_____ Postcode _____

Tel _____ Email _____

Total enclosed £ _____ (cheques should be made payable to 'BRF')

Please charge my Visa ☐ Mastercard ☐ Switch card ☐ with £ _____

Card no: ☐☐☐☐ ☐☐☐☐ ☐☐☐☐ ☐☐☐☐

Expires ☐☐☐☐   Security code ☐☐☐

Issue no (Switch only) ☐☐☐☐

Signature (essential if paying by credit/Switch) _____

GUIDELINES INDIVIDUAL SUBSCRIPTIONS

❏ I would like to take out a subscription myself:

Your name _____

Your address _____

_____ Postcode _____

Tel _____ Email _____

Please send *Guidelines* beginning with the May 2015 / September 2015 / January 2016 issue: (delete as applicable)

(please tick box)	UK	Europe/Economy	Standard
GUIDELINES	❏ £16.35	❏ £24.00	❏ £27.60
GUIDELINES 3-year sub	❏ £42.75		
GUIDELINES pdf download	❏ £12.90 (UK and overseas)		

Please complete the payment details below and send with appropriate payment to: **BRF, 15 The Chambers, Vineyard, Abingdon OX14 3FE**

Total enclosed £ _____ (cheques should be made payable to 'BRF')

Please charge my Visa ❏ Mastercard ❏ Switch card ❏ with £ _____

Card no: ☐☐☐☐☐☐☐☐☐☐☐☐☐☐☐☐☐☐☐☐

Expires ☐☐☐☐ Security code ☐☐☐

Issue no (Switch only) ☐☐☐☐

Signature (essential if paying by card) _____

To set up a direct debit, please also complete the form on page 159 and send it to BRF with this form.

GUIDELINES GIFT SUBSCRIPTIONS

❏ I would like to give a gift subscription (please provide both names and addresses:

Your name _____

Your address _____

_____ Postcode _____

Tel _____ Email _____

Gift subscription name _____

Gift subscription address _____

_____ Postcode _____

Gift message (20 words max. or include your own gift card for the recipient)

_____

_____

Please send *Guidelines* beginning with the May 2015 / September 2015 / January 2016 issue: (delete as applicable)

(please tick box)	UK	Europe/Economy	Standard
GUIDELINES	❏ £16.35	❏ £24.00	❏ £27.60
GUIDELINES 3-year sub	❏ £42.75		
GUIDELINES pdf download	❏ £12.90 (UK and overseas)		

Please complete the payment details below and send with appropriate payment to: **BRF, 15 The Chambers, Vineyard, Abingdon OX14 3FE**

Total enclosed £ _____ (cheques should be made payable to 'BRF')

Please charge my Visa ❏ Mastercard ❏ Switch card ❏ with £ _____

Card no: ⬜⬜⬜⬜ ⬜⬜⬜⬜ ⬜⬜⬜⬜ ⬜⬜⬜⬜ ⬜⬜⬜⬜

Expires ⬜⬜⬜⬜ Security code ⬜⬜⬜

Issue no (Switch only) ⬜⬜⬜⬜

Signature (essential if paying by card) _____

To set up a direct debit, please also complete the form on page 159 and send it to BRF with this form.

DIRECT DEBIT PAYMENTS

Now you can pay for your annual subscription to BRF notes using Direct Debit. You need only give your bank details once, and the payment is made automatically every year until you cancel it. If you would like to pay by Direct Debit, please use the form opposite, entering your BRF account number under 'Reference'.

You are fully covered by the Direct Debit Guarantee:

The Direct Debit Guarantee

- This Guarantee is offered by all banks and building societies that accept instructions to pay Direct Debits.
- If there are any changes to the amount, date or frequency of your Direct Debit, The Bible Reading Fellowship will notify you 10 working days in advance of your account being debited or as otherwise agreed. If you request The Bible Reading Fellowship to collect a payment, confirmation of the amount and date will be given to you at the time of the request.
- If an error is made in the payment of your Direct Debit, by The Bible Reading Fellowship or your bank or building society, you are entitled to a full and immediate refund of the amount paid from your bank or building society.
  - – If you receive a refund you are not entitled to, you must pay it back when The Bible Reading Fellowship asks you to.
- You can cancel a Direct Debit at any time by simply contacting your bank or building society. Written confirmation may be required. Please also notify us.

The Bible Reading Fellowship

Instruction to your bank or
building society to pay by Direct Debit

DIRECT Debit

Please fill in the whole form using a ballpoint pen and send to The Bible Reading Fellowship, 15 The Chambers, Vineyard, Abingdon OX14 3FE.

Service User Number: | 5 | 5 | 8 | 2 | 2 | 9 |

Name and full postal address of your bank or building society

To: The Manager	Bank/Building Society
Address	
	Postcode

Name(s) of account holder(s)

Branch sort code

| | | | | | |

Bank/Building Society account number

| | | | | | | | |

Reference

| | | | | | | | |

Instruction to your Bank/Building Society

Please pay The Bible Reading Fellowship Direct Debits from the account detailed in this instruction, subject to the safeguards assured by the Direct Debit Guarantee.
I understand that this instruction may remain with The Bible Reading Fellowship and, if so, details will be passed electronically to my bank/building society.

Signature(s)	
Date	

Banks and Building Societies may not accept Direct Debit instructions for some types of account.

This page is intentionally left blank.